OSPREY COMBAT AIRCR

US ARMY
AH-1 COBRA UNITS
IN VIETNAM

SERIES EDITOR: TONY HOLMES

OSPREY COMBAT AIRCRAFT • 41

US ARMY
AH-1 COBRA UNITS
IN VIETNAM

Jonathan Bernstein

OSPREY
PUBLISHING

Front cover
1Lt George Alexander and WO1 Jim Moran, flying AH-1G 68-15049 'Romeo 1', break hard right to bring their turret weapons to bear as 'Medevac 2' flares for touchdown and begins taking heavy automatic weapons fire from Viet Cong forces hidden in the treeline. Seconds later, 'Medevac 2's' tailboom would separate and the UH-1H (67-17485) would roll over, throwing medic SFC Louis Rocco clear of the crash. While 1Lt Alexander (callsign 'Precise Swords 12') and his wingmen, CW2 Paul Garrity and WO1 Jim Nabours ('Precise Swords 12A'), continued to lay suppressive minigun, 40 mm grenade and rocket fire on the now-visible bunkers along the treeline, SFC Rocco climbed back into the burning helicopter to rescue its crew. Finding Sgt Gary Taylor dead, Rocco managed to pull the remaining four crewmen to safety despite his own severe injuries.

Heavy fighting continued in the Landing Zone (LZ), and additional 'Blue Max' Cobras were called in to support the downed Medevac helicopter crew, as well as elements of the 9th ARVN (Army of the Republic of Vietnam) Airborne Brigade that were also pinned down in the area. Attempts to extract the downed crew and wounded ARVN paratroopers met with fierce resistance, severely damaging three more UH-1 Hueys before rescue efforts were suspended for the night.

On the ground, SFC Rocco organised the group's defence and kept his crew alive and alert until morning, when elements of the 229th Assault Helicopter Battalion, supported by 'Blue Max' Cobras, were able to pull them out.

Following his actions on 24-25 May 1970 at 'Medevac Meadow', SFC Louis Rocco was duly awarded the United State's highest military decoration, the Medal of Honor (*Cover artwork by Mark Postlethwaite*)

For a catalogue of all Osprey Publishing titles please contact us at:

Osprey Direct UK, PO Box 140, Wellingborough, Northants NN8 2FA, UK
E-mail: **info@ospreydirect.co.uk**

Osprey Direct USA, c/o MBI Publishing, 729 Prospect Ave, PO Box 1, Osceola, WI 54020, USA
E-mail: **info@ospreydirectusa.com**

First published in Great Britain in 2003 by Osprey Publishing
Elms Court, Chapel Way, Botley, Oxford, OX2 9LP

ISBN 1 84176 606 2

Edited by Tony Holmes
Page design by Tony Truscott
Cover Artwork by Mark Postlethwaite
Aircraft Profiles by Jim Laurier
Scale Drawings by Mark Styling
Index by Alan Thatcher
Orgination by Grasmere Digital Imaging., Leeds, UK
Printed in Singapore by Stamford Press PTE Ltd

03 04 05 06 07   10 9 8 7 6 5 4 3 2 1

EDITOR'S NOTE
To make this best-selling series as authoritative as possible, the Editor would be interested in hearing from any individual who may have relevant photographs, documentation or first-hand experiences relating to the world's elite pilots, and their aircraft, of the various theatres of war. Any material used will be credited to its original source. Please write to Tony Holmes via e-mail at: tony.holmes@osprey-jets.freeserve.co.uk

ACKNOWLEDGEMENTS
I would firstly like to thank the pilots and groundcrews who flew and worked on these magnificent machines in Vietnam. I have never worked with a more willing and generous group of people. The Vietnam Helicopter Pilots' Association has also been of great assistance in helping me put this book together, and I would like to thank Gary Roush and John Conway for their support. The Vietnam archive at Texas Tech University has provided me with much information, as well as support, and special thanks to Dr Ron Frankum, Steve Maxner and Dr James Reckner for granting me access to this material. A sincere thank you also to Malcolm Laing of the Texas Air Museum for 'giving a kid a shot' all those years ago, and to Jeff Herne of the New Jersey Aviation Hall of Fame for allowing me unfettered access to AH-1G 69-16437 *Heather Dawn* for 'hands-on' experience with the Cobra. Finally, thanks to my family and friends, who have put up with my passion for military aviation. I could not have gotten here without your ever-present support.

The Editor would like to thank Mike Verier for the provision of original Bell line artwork, which was in turn used by Mark Styling to ensure the accuracy of his finished scale drawings.

CONTENTS

DEVELOPMENT

With the convening of the Howze Board in 1962, the era of US Army helicopter-borne warfare had truly begun. The use of helicopters for 'vertical envelopment' through air mobility perfectly suited these new machines, which had in turn given the Army an unparalleled degree of combat flexibility in the post-Korean War era. Gen Hamilton Howze's Board presented its findings to the Army on 30 August 1962, and it recommended the creation of new 'Air Cavalry' combat brigades, and the design of specific aircraft for use by these new units. The new 'Sky Cav' doctrine, created by the 11th Air Assault Division and perfected by them in the jungles of the Republic of Vietnam as the 1st Cavalry Division, would change the face of warfare forever.

The early years of the Vietnam War clearly showed that while the doctrine was sound, the equipment being used by the Army could be improved. Bolting weapons onto UH-1A, B and C model Hueys to create gunships to escort troop-carrying helicopters and support troops on the ground was adequate, and from 1962, these aircraft performed the gunship mission very effectively through to the end of the conflict. However, while they were able to do the job, the limitations of these helicopters were readily apparent to both the crews and to the Army at large. The Huey gunships possessed plenty of firepower, but were underpowered and too slow to effectively escort and protect the larger, faster CH-47 Chinook – the standard medium lift helicopter employed by the US Army in Vietnam.

Thus dawned the age of the attack helicopter. The engineers at Bell Helicopter, acutely aware of the future need for a machine of this

Bell's first attempt at a pure attack helicopter was the D255 Iroquois Warrior, seen here in 1962. The family resemblance to the UH-1 is readily apparent when looking at the tailboom. Although it was a radical departure from previous helicopter designs, and had a great deal of development potential, the Army was not interested in the D255 project (*Bell*)

The OH-13X Sioux Scout was an 'off-the-shelf' concept demonstrator. Pilots who flew it liked the little machine, and were excited about the idea of a bigger, faster and more powerful version (*Bell*)

type, designed a futuristic mockup of a potential contender for the world's first true attack helicopter. Unveiled to the Army in June 1962 at Bell's Fort Worth, Texas, facility, the D255 Iroquois Warrior, as the company-funded project was known, met with a mix of awe and scepticism. Conservative elements within the army saw little need for such a sophisticated and, as yet, unproven helicopter. Proponents viewed the machine as one that could move with near impunity over the modern battlefield.

While the D255 was certainly an impressive sight, a great deal of research and development was needed to validate Bell's concept before a prototype could be built. The decision was made to create a flying testbed to prove the principles of armed helicopter doctrine. A hybrid aircraft was duly created utilising the proven Bell H-13 as the basis for the design. This small helicopter, famous for its service as an air ambulance in the Korean War, was the ideal platform to illustrate this concept.

Using the tailboom of a Model 47-J mated to a completely redesigned fuselage, Bell created the Model 207, also known as the OH-13X Sioux Scout. This new aircraft incorporated several features that would become standard on attack helicopter designs for the next 40 years. A tandem, stepped cockpit was added instead of the usual side-by-side seating, the pilot being sat in the rear seat, which was slightly higher than the gunner in front of him. This was done to allow an all-around view for both crewmembers, and also to ensure that the helicopter had as small a frontal silhouette as possible.

Flight-testing of the single testbed Model 207 (carrying civilian register N73927) commenced in 1963, and pilots who flew the helicopter were suitably impressed, although they all wanted an aircraft with more power and capability. The General Electric TAT-101 turret performed well, and its twin M-60 machine guns functioned properly. This turret validated the helicopter as a flexible gun platform, and would later be seen on US Marine Corps UH-1E gunships in Vietnam.

COMPETITION

In 1964, the US Army initiated the Advanced Aerial Fire Support System (AAFSS) competition in order to fund the development of a helicopter with superior troop carrier escort and ground support capabilities. Bell redesigned its Model D255 and created the updated Model D262. The design still incorporated numerous features from the UH-1, including the tailboom, drive train and rotor system. The D262 was an intimidating looking machine that appeared to have more in common with a craft from the 'Buck Rogers' comic strip than previous Bell helicopter designs! The other two entrants in the AAFSS competition were the Sikorsky S-66 and the Lockheed CL-840, both of which were radical designs that incorporated a pusher propeller at the rear of the aircraft to increase speed. The Bell design did not include this feature, and was eliminated early in the competition.

The Lockheed design was declared the winner in the spring of 1965, and development was begun on the AH-56 Cheyenne. Bell's engineers had realised early on that the development period for the AAFSS would be considerable, and that a viable combat aircraft would not arrive in Vietnam for some time. An interim gunship would be needed until the AAFSS was ready for combat, and with this in mind, Bell's Experimental Projects department turned its attention to a privately funded company venture – the Model D209. This helicopter retained a large degree of commonality with the Huey, as had Bell's preceding attack helicopter mockups, but was considerably more refined.

Design work by consultant Richard Ten Eyke, formerly of Cessna Aircraft, began in February 1965, and a prototype was completed

The Model D262 was Bell's entry for the US Army's Advanced Aerial Fire Support System competition. Like the D255, the D262's Huey family resemblance is apparent in the tailboom. The design was disqualified before a prototype could be constructed (*Bell*)

within seven months – a remarkably short gestation period for a modern combat aircraft! The D209 incorporated proven concepts from the Model D207, as well as features of both the D255 and D262. The end result was the creation of an entirely new aircraft, which made use of the engine, drive train and rotor system of the UH-1C gunships that were currently being fielded in Vietnam.

While the design and construction of the D209 was coming to fruition, the US Army announced the need for an interim gunship, and convened the 'Bush Board' under Col Harry Bush of Army Materiel Command to choose a viable candidate. On 18 August 1965, Bell engineers presented the Model D209 concept to the board as a development of the UH-1B, and not as the new design that it was.

The prototype, which came to be known by its civilian registration N209J, was completed ahead of schedule and only $40,000 over budget. Design and construction went smoothly, although some minor problems were encountered. The biggest difficulty centred on deciding on the landing gear configuration, and whether retractable skids offered any significant aerodynamic improvement over fixed gear. The prototype was built with retractable skids, but all subsequent Cobra landing gear would be of the fixed type so as to save on construction time, reduce complexity and avoid unnecessary systems taking up space inside an already cramped airframe.

The prototype was rolled out of the special projects hangar on 2 September 1965, and within two days it was complete and ready to begin flight testing. The first ground run took place on 7 September, and the first flight of the new 'UH-1' model was made that same afternoon, with Bell test pilot Bill Quinlan at the controls.

With its fuselage being a mere 38 inches wide, the D209 presented an extremely small target area when viewed head-on. Its primary weapons system was a GAU-2B/A (M-134) 7.62 mm minigun, housed in a streamlined turret under the nose. And while the D209 had stub wings, it lacked the underwing pylons that would give production Cobras their impressive load-carrying capability. Indeed, production models would have the ability to carry up to four 2.75-in Folding Fin Aerial Rockets (FFARs) pods, each of which contained 19 rounds.

The US Army was impressed with the D209, and it began flight testing with Bell Helicopter on 23 September 1965. Gen George P Seneff was the first Army officer to fly the machine, and he gave it an enthusiastic endorsement after his flight. Testing was moved to Edwards Air Force Base in California in November, and then to Fort Sill, Oklahoma, in December. During this period, the Army was also evaluating the Kaman UH-2 and Piasecki 16H designs as possible interim gunship platforms. It was clear, however,

Bell's Model D209 served as the Cobra prototype. Seen here on an early test flight, the N209J was a company-funded testbed using the drivetrain and tailboom from a UH-1B to create a completely new aircraft. Note the helicopter's unique retractable landing skids (*Bell*)

that the Model D209 held a significant edge over the competition.

A $20.5 million contract was awarded to Bell Helicopter for the Cobra on 4 April 1966, this covering the provision of two pre-production and 110 production aircraft, which would be designated AH-1Gs by the Army. Although some modifications were made, these airframes would be very similar in appearance to the original Model D209. The principal changes were as follows: fittings for the weapons turret housing were

enlarged to accommodate the Emerson Electric TAT-102A turret; the stub wings were made bigger so as to allow the carriage of ordnance pylons; the ventral fin was removed; and fixed-tube landing skids replaced the retractable ones.

The two pre-production aircraft, serials 66-15246 and '247 respectively, were built by hand using the same methods as the Model D209, and incorporating the aforementioned modifications to allow for the proper testing of production components. 66-15246 was completed in October 1966, and it was immediately designated as the armament qualifications airframe and sent to Fort Hood, in Texas, to complete this test phase. 66-15247, which flew for the first time in March 1967, was used to test the new Stabilization Control Augmentation System (SCAS) that replaced the perpendicular stabiliser bar on the 540 'door hinge' rotor system.

This second helicopter, even though it was a pre-production test airframe, subsequently became one of six AH-1s to be selected for the New Equipment Training Team – a combined Army/Bell unit that was to train air and groundcrews in Vietnam on the new helicopter. The AH-1 was on the verge of winning its battle spurs.

Skids extended, the N209J prototype prepares to land. This machine was the only Cobra to be built with retractable skids, Bell initially following this route in order to achieve maximum streamlining for its new attack helicopter, thus boosting its top speed. It was also felt that a greater turret arc would be possible with the skids out of the way. However, fixed skids were eventually adopted in order to avoid the extra weight and complexity involved with fitting the retraction gear. The helicopter's top speed was not drastically affected by the fixed skids, and the crash-worthiness of a damaged aircraft was also increased when they were fitted. Finally, it was felt that an average service pilot would, at some point, fail to remember that the retracted skids were not 'down and welded', and land on the helicopter's belly! (*Bell*)

Cobra 'techreps' and New Equipment Training Team (NETT) crew chiefs work on one of the first six Cobras to arrive in South Vietnam, at Bien Hoa, in September 1967. According to several NETT crew chiefs like SP4 Jessie Robertson, 'nothing transferred from aircraft to aircraft. Each of these first birds was unique!' (*Jessie Robertson*)

1967 – BEGINNINGS

The USAF C-141 carrying Lt Col Paul Anderson's New Equipment Training Team (NETT) arrived at Bien Hoa Air Force Base in the early afternoon of 29 August 1967. Upon landing, the nearly 50 officers, enlisted and civilian technicians began preparations for the delivery of the unit's aircraft and equipment, which would arrive at the air base on the outskirts of Saigon a short time later. The AH-1s were being flown in by four fully loaded C-133 Cargomasters, these older aircraft being selected to transport the first Cobras overseas because they could accommodate the helicopters' rotor masts – they possessed greater overhead space than the ubiquitous C-130.

Once the unit's 12 AH-1Gs were offloaded from their transports NETT technicians set about re-attaching rotor assemblies and checking systems on the helicopters. Six of these aircraft would stay with NETT, while the remaining six would transfer to the 'Playboy' platoon of the 334th Assault Helicopter Company (AHC) upon the unit's completion of the first Cobra transition class. Among the six NETT-assigned aircraft was 66-15247, the second pre-production Cobra. This machine, and the first three production aircraft, was completely hand-built. Commonality was a problem with these aircraft, and according to several crew chiefs like SP4 Jessie Robertson, 'Nothing transferred from aircraft to aircraft. Each of these first birds was unique!'

A NETT crew chief works on the Lycoming T53-L-13 engine fitted to one of the recently arrived Cobras in the late afternoon sun at Bien Hoa in September 1967 (*Jessie Robertson*)

AH-1G 66-15259 *"Virginia Rose II"* sits in a revetment at Bien Hoa, looking resplendent in its unusual three-colour white/tan/olive finish. It was one of two early NETT AH-1s to be sprayed up in-country using USAF paint stocks held at Bien Hoa. It fell to 66-15259 to complete the first AH-1 flight in South Vietnam on 4 September 1967 (*VHPA*)

Helicopter flightsuit heraldry truly blossomed during the Vietnam conflict, and the Cobra community produced its fair share of memorable motifs. This was the 'grand daddy' of all AH-1 unit emblems – the Cobra NETT patch (*Author's collection*)

This Bell Helicopter pamphlet commemorates the first anniversary of the Cobra in combat, highlighting the kills made during Gen George Seneff's orientation flight on 4 September 1967 (*Bell*)

Rearmed, refuelled and ready for action, a 334th AHC 'Playboy' platoon AH-1G sits on the Bien Hoa steel matting in October 1967. The helicopter is armed with 19-shot XM-200 rocket pods (housing 2.75-in FFARs) on the outer stub hardpoints and XM-18 Minigun pods (each containing a single 7.62 mm six-barrelled machine gun, complete with 1500 rounds of ammunition) inboard (*Jessie Robertson*)

The anticipated arrival of the Cobra sparked a great deal of interest from around Vietnam, and the type's first in-country flight was a somewhat public event. On 4 September, in front of Gen Westmoreland, commander of US forces in Vietnam, and Gen George Seneff, commander of the 1st Aviation Brigade, the Cobra made its first in-country flight. At 1707 hrs local time, AH-1G 66-15259 lifted off from Bien Hoa, with Lt Col Anderson piloting and Maj Nicolas P Stein, NETT Maintenance Officer, as co-pilot.

'We basically offloaded the helicopters and set about getting them ready to fly', stated Maj Stein, this first flight being short and, according to the major, 'a simple "dog and pony show" to let everyone know that we'd arrived'. The aircraft, nicknamed *"Virginia Rose II"*, wore an experimental paint scheme more reminiscent of current USAF colours than the overall olive drab that the Army was so familiar with, and 66-15259 retained its unique white/tan/olive scheme throughout its tour of duty in Southeast Asia.

Gen Seneff, who was instrumental in getting the Cobra put into production and sent to Vietnam, got the opportunity to fly one on 4 September. His orientation sortie would make history, as the helicopter's first combat kill was claimed during the course of the flight.

NETT had despatched a Cobra to Muc Hoa, in IV Corps, as a show of force in order to make it known to the locals that the AH-1 had arrived. Although no action was expected, the aircraft was nevertheless loaded with two XM-200 19-shot rocket pods, two XM-18 minigun pods and 2000 rounds of 7.62 mm ammunition for the turret minigun. CW2 John D Thomson commanded the aircraft, with Gen Seneff flying in the front seat.

The mission was supposed to be a routine flight, with no enemy activity expected. However, the Viet Cong (VC) had other intentions, and at around 1100 hrs a sampan was discovered in a 'free-fire zone' on the Mekong River with four suspect figures aboard. When closer inspection of the craft revealed that the occupants were armed, Gen Seneff gave the order to attack. A combination of rocket and minigun fire sank the sampan and claimed a body count of four VC – the first combat kills for the Cobra.

Two days later, at Bien Hoa, Gen Westmoreland was briefed on

the Cobra's capabilities, after which he was given a colourful display of its potential during a flying demonstration. For the remainder of the month NETT concentrated on qualifying pilots and ground-crews from the 'Playboy Platoon' of the 334th. The first class graduated from NETT Cobra transition on 4 October, and the six AH-1s passed onto the 334th became operational two days later.

Combat sorties commenced on 8 October when two 334th Cobras left Tan Son Nhut Air Force Base at 0625 hrs and

A 1966-contract 'minigun-ship' is viewed head on. It too is fitted with 19-shot XM-200 pods outboard and XM-18 Minigun pods inboard – the latter could be fired at a devastating 4000 rounds per minute. All early-build AH-1s boasted twin landing lights in the extreme nose, and these were later replaced by a belly-mounted retractable unit (*Author's collection*)

leapfrogged to their forward operating base at Duc Hoa, some 20 miles west of Saigon. The day's missions would provide a taste of what lay in store for AH-1 pilots over the next six years.

They were first tasked to perform a visual reconnaissance (VR) towards the Cambodian border. Once airborne, Capt Ken Rubin, in 'Playboy 16', was contacted by an Army 0-1 Bird Dog flying nearby. Three sampans had been discovered partially concealed in the weeds along a canal. Capt Rubin and his wingman, CW2 Robert Bey, made one pass over the area to assess the situation. Not finding any movement around the sampans, Rubin and Bey rolled in, and in two passes destroyed all three vessels. The fire team continued reconnaissance operations in the area, discovering and destroying four more sampans, before heading to Tan An to refuel and rearm.

From Tan An, the Cobra crews were then tasked with escorting ten UH-1Ds of the 118th Assault Helicopter Company (AHC). The Command and Control (C&C) Huey informed Capt Rubin of the Landing Zone (LZ) location, that there were no 'friendlies' in the area and that fire had been received from the tree line.

The original cadre of 334th AHC 'Playboy' platoon pilots pose in their flamboyant, custom-made flightsuits. Like fighter pilots, the Cobra crews cultivated a certain 'style' in Vietnam that reflected the elite nature of their combat operations. These men are, back row, from left to right, WO1s Dodson, Ulsh, Dawson, Wydur and Roger S Cameron (the first AH-1 crewman killed in action in Vietnam on 1 February 1968 at My Tho), and front row, from left to right, WO1 Welch, Capt Ken Rubin and WO1 Bey (*Ken Rubin*)

The fire team's initial pass began at 3000 ft over the LZ, each Cobra unleashing 15 pairs of rockets into the tree line and hundreds of rounds of 7.62 mm minigun fire. Upon pulling out, the AH-1 crews could clearly see bunkers in the tree line. They then worked a racetrack pattern over the tree line at approximately 1500 ft, Capt Rubin launching another 15 pairs of rockets at the bunkers, while CW2 Bey cleared the tree line at the approach end of the LZ. Each Cobra made one more pass, utilising the belly smoke grenade dispenser to mark the centre of the

LZ with violet smoke. Rubin then radioed the following message to the incoming 'Slicks' (UH-1s);

'Lead, this is 1-6. LZ is HOT. Suggest you land from east to west. Winds calm. Fire received and reported on the south side of the LZ. Suggest you take off to the west with an immediate right break. Over.'

As the 'Slicks' flared for touchdown, the two Cobras emptied their miniguns into the tree line to suppress any enemy fire. The American advisor with the South Vietnamese unit that was being lifted into the LZ later commented that not a single enemy round was fired at them during the landing. Thirteen enemy bodies were found, along with two 0.51-cal machine guns. The Cobra's combat debut had been stellar, but questions remained about its survivability under intense enemy anti-aircraft fire.

Throughout October 1967, the 334th continued to fly close air support, reconnaissance and escort missions in the III Corps area of responsibility. On 22 October, the unit's Cobras flew for the first time in support of the 7th Battalion, Royal Australian Regiment. Two Cobras from the 'Playboy' platoon, flown by Maj Donald Becker and WO Larry Welch, moved from Bien Hoa to Nui Dat to offer close support to the Australian Task Force. It was believed that the VC were virtually finished in the province, and that pacification operations undertaken by Allied troops would be able to clear out the remaining pockets of resistance. The following months would prove this assumption very wrong.

On 16 November the Cobra's run of unopposed sorties came to an end when Capt Rubin, who was flying 66-15272 on an escort mission for the 118th AHC, came under intense 0.30-cal fire. The helicopter was hit five times, one bullet piercing a wiring bundle which then illuminated a fire warning light on his control panel.

Unsure of whether or not the engine was on fire, Capt Rubin set the aircraft down as soon as possible. After inspecting bullet hits in the ammunition compartment, fuel cell and the electrical systems, the Cobra was slung under a CH-47 and flown back to Bien Hoa for repairs. It was later determined that the damage to the wiring bundle had indeed caused a short which illuminated the warning light.

As a result of this mission, Bell Helicopter relocated the wiring bundle that was severed to an armoured position inside the engine compartment on all subsequent Cobras, thus ensuring no repeat of this incident in the future. Both the VC and the North Vietnamese Army (NVA) were fast learning how to deal with the Cobra in combat, anti-aircraft fire growing more intense and accurate when the AH-1s were in the area.

On 8 December 1967, the 30th and 38th ARVN Ranger battalions initiated combat assault operations southeast of Phu Cong. The ARVN element moving west encountered stiff resistance after advancing just 400 metres along the small north-south stream line, resulting in two medevac ('Dustoff') missions being requested for 11 wounded in action and one killed. 'Dustoff' attempted to land at the position by flying in at low level, but the enemy fire was so heavy that they had to abort the mission. Both aircraft were hit, with one crew chief taking a round in his 'chicken plate' body armour, which saved his life. While providing cover for medical evacuation, an armed helicopter fire team, comprised of UH-1Cs from the 68th AHC, was taken under heavy fire – one helicopter was hit, forcing it to return to base for repairs. Meanwhile, an Army Forward Air Controller (FAC) from the 74th Reconnaissance Aeroplane Company (RAC) directed artillery and air strikes upon the enemy positions.

A fire team from the 334th AHC relieved the stricken 68th UH-1Cs and joined the fray, concentrating their fire on the enemy automatic weapons positions. Reports indicate that one of the Cobras was hit during a pass and the pilot severely wounded, although available records were not able to corroborate this. Some six helicopters sustained damage during the course of the action, one of which required evacuation by CH-47, two were repaired for a one-time flight to base and three were undamaged. Both Cobras that participated in the engagement were also apparently hit, although they were able to stay on station and keep firing on the target until the enemy positions were neutralised.

On 14 December the 'Playboys' were called out to support the 190th AHC, which had been assigned to support Company A, 5th Special Forces Group (CIDG) in airmobile operations in the area west of Hiep Hoa, in South Vietnam. On the final approach to the LZ, the flight was subjected to

A close-up view of the M-134 Minigun installation in the original TAT-102A turret. This was the primary weapon of the early AH-1Gs sent to Vietnam (*Russell Stewart*)

AH-1G 66-15275 is seen undergoing routine maintenance on its left 7.62 mm Minigun. Again, the fairing that covered the weapon when in flight has been removed. Note the fully loaded XM-200 pod on the outer stub pylon (*Jessie Robertson*)

'Playboy' platoon pilots repair components from the TAT-102 turret/M-134 Minigun fitted to one of the unit's newly-arrived Cobras. The AH-1G has already been adorned with the unit's *PLAYBOY* titling and insignia (*Jessie Robertson*)

light automatic weapons fire and one helicopter was hit, damaging its hydraulic system and wounding the crew chief. An hour after the insertions, the ground unit made contact with an estimated regimental-sized force. Tactical air and two light fire teams from the 190th provided immediate support, although the enemy was well entrenched, and possessed an estimated six 0.51-cal machine guns. The fire from these weapons was devastating, and fire support to assist the CIDG's disengagement was a dire necessity.

A 'Playboy' fire team was scrambled from Bien Hoa, arriving on-station in moments and raining down rockets and minigun fire. This was the first time Cobras were challenged by the heavy firepower of 0.51-cal weapons. However, the efforts of the AH-1s, combined with those of the UH-1C gunship crews of the 190th, enabled the CIDG company to disengage to a safe LZ from where they could be airlifted out.

Three of the UH-1Cs were hit during the engagement, with one of them being damaged so badly that its pilot had to autorotate to an emergency landing. Although the sky was filled with enemy fire, the downed aircraft's wingman landed through the hail of bullets to pull the crew practically out of the enemy's hands. The action of the Cobras in the face of superior enemy firepower made the difference between friendly units on the ground being destroyed and successfully withdrawal. The 190th AHC had two crewmembers wounded, one UH-1C gunship totally destroyed and three others damaged.

On 31 December the Meritorious Unit Citation was awarded to the 145th Combat Aviation Battalion and its sub-units, the 68th, 118th and 334th AHCs, for operations conducted in 1967. During this time period the 334th AHC had become the first Vietnam-based unit to operate the AH-1G in combat, and its crews had developed many of the tactics that would be used by Cobra crews over the next six years.

1968 –
TRIAL BY FIRE

Gen Westmoreland's 'light at the end of the tunnel' speech, concerning the war's imminent outcome in favour of the South Vietnamese, and their US allies, was proven woefully wrong in the pre-dawn hours of 31 January 1968. VC and NVA units attacked major cities and American bases across South Vietnam, breaking the planned Tet holiday ceasefire.

The Tet Offensive, launched in the pre-dawn hours of 31 January 1968, saw numerous US base in South Vietnam come under direct attack by VC and NVA forces. Bien Hoa, home to the 'Playboy' platoon and the Cobra NETT, was amongst those targeted, this photograph being taken soon after the attack was launched. It shows smoke rising from the nearby USAF ammunition dump at Long Binh, which VC sappers infiltrated and destroyed (*Jessie Robertson*)

At around 0300 hrs local time, Bien Hoa was hit hard by 122 mm rocket and mortar fire, immediately after which elements of three VC regiments attacked the base between the 101st Airborne cantonment and III Corps HQ on the eastern side of the airfield. Their objective was to destroy as many aircraft and cause as much damage as possible. USAF Security Police initially held off the enemy incursions, but they were soon overwhelmed and fighting for their lives at 'Bunker Hill 10', which was the main perimeter strongpoint on that side of the base.

Upon hearing the impact of the first mortar rounds, the 'Playboy' groundcrews scrambled to the flightline to get the platoon's idle Cobras armed, pre-flighted and ready for take-off. Two AH-1s that were already on a 'Firefly' night mission to Duc Hoa, southwest of Saigon, were ordered to return immediately. They would prove to be

The 334th AHC's enlisted barracks at Bien Hoa in early 1968 (*Jessie Robertson*)

Spent ammunition boxes lay in a pile on the 'Playboy' flightline on the morning of 31 January 1968 after the unit had spent several hours battling VC infiltrators who had succeeded in overrunning the eastern end of Bien Hoa (*Jessie Robertson*)

SP4 Jessie Robertson works on the rotor hub of 66-15272 in the autumn of 1967. Robertson was in the first class to graduate from Cobra transition school at Bien Hoa in September of that year (*Jessie Robertson*)

instrumental in the defence of Bien Hoa. The unit's remaining pilots, were quartered in a hotel on Cong Li Street in downtown Bien Hoa City, about a mile from the base, and after some initial confusion, several jeeps arrived to transport the 334th pilots to the flightline with minimal delay.

In a classic case of bad timing, elements of the VC's 274th, 275th and 68th Infantry Regiments launched their attack just as Capt Rubin's 'Firefly' mission returned to base. Informed by the C&C Huey on station over the airfield that the base was under attack, Capt Rubin turned AH-1G 66-15275 towards the eastern side of the base to support the USAF security personnel pinned down at 'Bunker Hill 10' and battling the onrushing VC. Making his first pass to assess the situation, Capt Rubin flew low over the VC positions to draw fire, enabling other gunships to then target the enemy.

VC were clearly visible firing back at the Cobras as they rolled in and raked the field with minigun and rocket fire. The AH-1s remained on station over 'Bunker Hill 10' for 30 minutes, expending all of their ordnance and suffering several hits in the process. Both Capt Rubin and his gunner were wounded, although not seriously enough to stop them from securing another AH-1 and returning to 'Bunker Hill 10' to further assist the security force battling to keep the VC at bay.

As daylight came, more hostile positions were discovered and attacked, with similar results. Capt Rubin, now flying with Col R Y McBurney (the USAF's Assistant Ops Officer at Bien Hoa) as his front-seater, was made aware of two wounded USAF guards caught in the open between enemy forces. While directing the other 'Playboy' Cobras in his team to suppress the surrounding enemy positions, Rubin performed the first medevac mission conducted by a Cobra – one that would be repeated countless times across Vietnam over the next six years. He landed and instructed the wounded men to open the AH-1's ammunition bay doors and climb onto them. Once aboard, they were then flown the short distance to safety. Rubin then returned to the scene and coordinated with ground security forces as they swept the area and wiped out the remaining resistance. He was subsequently awarded the Distinguished Service Cross (DSC) for his actions on this morning.

Later that day 'Snakes' from the 334th were despatched to support ground units operating in III

Literally thousands of 2.75-in FFAR rockets, fitted with 10-lb warheads, were expended in just a matter of hours by AH-1G fire teams in the opening battles of the Tet Offensive. This trolley would have been hastily wheeled over to a returning Cobra and its cargo slotted into empty XM-159 pods within minutes of the AH-1G having shut down on the Bien Hoa ramp. Other maintainers would have been simultaneously reloading the minigun pods and the TAT-102A turret while the helicopter's fuel tanks were replenished (*Jessie Robertson*)

Corps. Fire team leader WO1 Roger S Cameron was sent to My Tho to escort UH-1s from another unit that were dropping supplies to the surrounded American Batchelor Officers' Quarters (BOQ) there. Cameron made several passes before taking fire from a 0.51-cal machine gun downtown. Realising the threat, he concentrated his fire on this position. However, fire from a second 0.51-cal weapon that the VC had set up on a rooftop caught his Cobra in heavy crossfire. WO1 Cameron became the first AH-1 crewman killed in action in Vietnam when he was struck by several heavy calibre rounds. His co-pilot was able to regain control of the helicopter before it hit the ground, and he duly returned to base.

The 334th Cobras, under Capt Rubin's command, were instrumental in repulsing the initial attacks on Bien Hoa. And although the mortars and rockets wrecked a number of aircraft at the base and destroyed the ammunition dump at Long Binh, the damage would have been far worse had the 'Playboys' not responded quickly to the threat.

With missions being flown from Bien Hoa throughout the day in opposition to the Tet attacks, NETT's Col Anderson and Maj Jarrett requested permission to assist in the defence of the base in an effort to take some pressure off the handful of 334th crews who were by then all but exhausted. Since NETT was not officially a combat unit, permission had to be granted by the commander of the 145th Combat Aviation Battalion for it to enter the fray, and this was quickly received. By late morning the combined efforts of the 'Playboy' platoon and NETT, along with the UH-1C gunship platoon of the 68th AHC 'Mustangs', had beaten back the main assault on Bien Hoa. However, a full 36 hours of non-stop combat would pass before

Capt Ken Rubin is congratulated by Lt Col Robert Deets, commander of the 145th Combat Aviation Battalion, after being awarded a DFC with Oak Leaf Cluster, Bronze Star, Air Medal and Purple Heart for his actions on 31 January 1968 (*Ken Rubin*)

AH-1 pilots and groundcrews were given a reprieve from flying support missions during Tet.

MORE COBRAS ARRIVE

While the 'Playboy' and NETT Cobras were busy in III Corps, the 235th Aero Weapons Company (AWC) was also flying its first combat missions in January 1968 from Can Tho, in IV Corps. The 235th 'Delta Devils' had arrived in Vietnam in November 1967, and had received its first Cobras by the end of the following month. Those pilots not qualified to fly the

A 3rd Platoon, 334th AHC UH-1C gunship speeds off on another mission over the eastern end of Bien Hoa on 31 January 1968. The remaining two platoons of the 334th would begin their conversion onto the Cobra by the summer of 1968, making the unit only the second Aeroweapons Company to see action in Vietnam (*Jessie Robertson*)

Cobra commenced their training programme with NETT in December, and they were flying their first combat missions in brand new aircraft by the second week of January 1968. The unit initially sortied mixed fire teams of one AH-1G and one UH-1C until it had enough pilots and machines on hand – the 235th had received 22 Cobras by Tet.

The 'Delta Devils' suffered their first casualty on 2 February when AH-1G 66-15309 was hit in the cockpit and forward doghouse by 0.30-cal machine gun fire. The aircraft commander was wounded in the engagement, although he survived.

The 235th AWC was the first unit in Vietnam to operate with a full complement of Cobras assigned, and although it flew other types in liaison and transport roles, the AH-1 was its primary weapon. The 'Delta Devils' were the only Cobra unit in IV Corps until the arrival of 7/1 Cavalry's AH-1s in July.

Support missions were flown round the clock for the 9th Infantry Division, and other US and ARVN units operating in the Mekong Delta, during the Tet Offensive, and although no AH-1s were destroyed during the bloody campaign, none of the 40 operational Cobras in-

The 235th AWC's (Attack Helicopter) Operations shack at Can Tho Army Air Field, in IV Corps. This unit had arrived in Vietnam in November 1967, and received its first AH-1Gs the following month. The 235th saw its first combat in January 1968 (*Roscoe Armstrong*)

theatre escaped unscathed. Indeed, all were hit by small arms and light anti-aircraft fire. The performance of the men and machines of the 334th, NETT and 235th during Tet proved that the Cobra could withstand damage and continue fighting.

At Bien Hoa, the 334th and Cobra NETT spent the remainder of February 1968 clearing pockets of resistance throughout Saigon, the AH-1 continuing to be devastatingly effective against VC infantry. The 235th, meanwhile,

OPERATIONS

235th AVN CO. (ATTACK HEL.)

AH-1G transition training in the US was conducted at the 'Cobra Hall' at Hunter-Stewart Army Air Field, Georgia. This class graduation photograph was taken in late 1968. The 'Hall' could crank out up to 40 trained crews every three weeks (*Robert Wiggins*)

The highly prized 'Cobra Hall' cap pin was awarded to graduates upon the completion of their course (*Robert Wiggins*)

persisted with its combat sorties in the Delta, participating in Operation *Truong Cong Dinh* from 1 March in support of the 9th Division in Dinh Truong and Kien Truong provinces. That same day the operational testing of the Cobra was declared complete and the helicopter deemed fully operational.

Late February and early March brought a major influx of new Cobras and qualified pilots to Vietnam. The NETT training programme was also able to qualify 12 new pilots and crew chiefs every two weeks, and these men, along with 40 'Cobra Hall'-trained personnel that arrived in-country every three weeks, began to fill the demand for AH-1 crews in the frontline. Problems were still encountered, however, for many of the units that Cobra-trained pilots were being assigned to had not yet received their aircraft, while units that had received their AH-1s suffered from a shortage of qualified pilots!

While the NETT training programme at Bien Hoa and 'Cobra Hall' at Hunter-Stewart Army Air Field, in Georgia, were training Cobra pilots at a rapid pace, it often fell on the units themselves to continue the conversion process in order to make up for the shortfall in qualified personnel. As a result of these manning problems, Instructor Pilots (IPs) in the frontline were tasked with providing familiarisation and conversion training for units that were unable to send pilots for dedicated in-country training. These IPs had the authorisation to give check-rides and sign off on a pilot's competency in the aircraft.

BACK ON THE OFFENSIVE

After Tet was declared over in February, US offensive operations resumed in earnest. The 1st Cavalry Division (Airmobile) had been in the middle of Operation *Jeb Stuart* when Tet started, and it continued its campaign whilst the communist offensive raged. In February, the division's first Cobras, assigned to 1/9 Cavalry and D Company of the

229th Assault Helicopter Battalion (AHB), began to arrive. By the second week of the month, 1st Cavalry AH-1s were conducting combat operations in I Corps, and meeting moderate resistance. The opening weeks proved to be fairly quiet, with the sole exception being a D/229 'Smiling Tigers' Cobra that was hit by AK-47 fire on the 23rd during an armed escort mission. Two holes in the tailboom and main rotor was the only damage inflicted.

However, the following week saw D/229 lose its first Cobra crew when a 'Firefly' mission took off from Camp Evans in heavy, low lying, cloud. CW2 Dale Fillmore ('Killer Spade 10') was the mission commander, flying one of two UH-1Hs that the 'Smiling Tigers' AH-1s were tasked with escorting. Both Hueys took off without difficulty, but were quickly in Instrument Flight Rules (IFR) conditions. Fillmore's crew chief then told his pilot that he had seen a massive glow beneath the clouds soon after the Cobras reported taking off. Radioing Evans Tower confirmed their suspicions that 'Smiling Tiger' Lead had gone down. 'Tiger Two' was able to abort its take off before flying into the fog. Both Cobra crewmen, 1Lt Gary N Shy and WO1 Russell L Wallace, were killed in the crash of AH-1G 66-15347, thus becoming the first Cobra and complete crew lost in Vietnam.

One of the first problems encountered with the Cobra in operational service was possibly the cause of this accident. Early AH-1s had a bluish tint to their canopy glass, which reduced the sun's glare during the day, but decreased outside visibility while increasing interior glare at night. In foggy weather, the glare could increase significantly enough to disorient the crew and allow them to fly into the ground.

The first week of March was equally troublesome for the 235th at Can Tho. On the 5th, 66-15293 came under intense AK-47 fire and received hits to its self-sealing fuel tank. The helicopter developed a fuel leak and its crew force-landed. The resulting structural damage rendered the aircraft unflyable, and it had to be lifted out by Chinook. The AH-1 was eventually sent back to Bell Helicopter for rebuilding and it would not return to Vietnam.

Two days later, another 235th aircraft (66-15320) was lost to enemy fire. The unit had sent in a fire team to attack NVA troops on the ground from 300 ft at a speed of 110 knots, and when numerous AK-47 rounds hit 66-15320, its pilot attempted an emergency autorotation landing but the aircraft was destroyed in the resulting crash. The 235th AWC had suffered its first loss.

AIR CAV

While units like the 229th AHB, 235th AWC and 334th AHC operated in fire teams of two AH-1s, which functioned in a close air support (CAS) and armed escort role, 1/9 Cav utilised the Cobra in a significantly different manner. Its primary mission was reconnaissance, resulting in the development of the 'hunter-killer' team. Such an outfit consisted of a single Cobra from the 'red', or gun platoon, and an OH-6 scout helicopter from the troop's 'white', or scout platoon. The resulting 'Pink Team' was ideally suited to 1/9 Cav's recce tasking.

The 'Pink Team' set up allowed the OH-6 to operate at low level, looking for signs of enemy activity in a particular Area of Operations, with significant firepower on hand in case of trouble. Once the scout began taking fire, the Cobra would roll in and fire its minigun and rockets at the target. All Air Cavalry squadrons operating in Vietnam would eventually adopt this formation.

KHE SANH

At the beginning of April 1968, the 1st Cavalry Division initiated Operation *Pegasus* into northwestern I Corps in an effort to relieve the besieged US Marine Corps base at Khe Sanh, which had been surrounded for two months. The operation consisted of leapfrogging combat assaults on each side of Route 9, running westward from the coast, and systematically reopening the road to the base. 'Pink Teams' from 1/9 Cav led the way, locating suitable LZs and discovering several large weapons caches left behind by the withdrawing NVA. 1/9 Cav's mission was also essential in locating enemy anti-aircraft positions before the main helicopter assault force commenced operations. During the early stages of *Pegasus*, a Cobra from C Troop was hit by AK-47 fire, which damaged the hydraulics and holed the main rotor, causing a severe vibration. The pilot managed to set the aircraft down, and he made sure that it was flyable prior to returning to base.

B Troop lost half of a 'Pink Team' on 7 April, when 1Lt Fred McMurray was downed in his OH-13S (s/n 63-9084) while conducting a visual reconnaissance mission. McMurray had sortied with a single AH-1G from the gun platoon, the pair heading west towards Thon Khe Xeng after departing LZ Stud. The OH-13 pilot, operating at low level, reported spotting newly repaired automatic weapons positions and signs of recent use on several trails. As McMurray marked the target with a smoke grenade, he sighted NVA soldiers and engaged them.

AH-1G 66-15316 also rolled in and began placing minigun and rocket fire on the target. Continuing to engage the enemy, the Cobra crew radioed LZ Stud to have the Aero Rifle platoon insert troops to conduct a ground assault on the enemy position. During the firefight, Lt McMurray's helicopter suffered numerous hits and began to burn in flight, before hitting the ground hard. McMurray's gunner, Sgt James Powers, was quickly picked up, but it was believed that McMurray was still in the helicopter. The next morning the Aero Rifle platoon was inserted in order to recover the pilot's body, but all they found was his 'chicken plate' armour and helmet neatly stacked. The enemy positions were soon neutralised and a number of enemy Killed By Air (KBA) were detected, although Lt McMurray's body was never found.

Throughout *Pegasus*, the 'Smiling Tigers' of D/229th AHB, along with 1st Cav's artillery division, prepped the LZs with massive amounts of firepower. Both 10- and 17-lb high explosive (HE) warheads were used on the Cobras' 2.75-in FFARs – the effect that 76 of these rockets had when they impacted a landing zone was truly devastating. After prepping the LZs, D Company Cobras remained over the landing zone and protected the incoming troop-carrying UH-1H 'Slicks', suppressing any further enemy activity and expending any remaining ammunition. After encountering light to moderate opposition during *Pegasus*, Khe Sanh was officially relieved by elements of 1st Cav on 8 April, thus ending the 77-day siege.

THE A SHAU VALLEY

The North Vietnamese infiltration of the South continued, despite setbacks following Tet. US planners knew that the Ho Chi Minh Trail passed through both Laos and Cambodia, and then snaked back into South Vietnam at various points throughout the country. Operation *Delaware* was initiated in mid-April 1968 in an effort to strangle those routes that re-entered South Vietnam from Laos in the northwestern corner the country.

The 1st Cavalry Division launched offensive operations into the A Shau Valley on 13 April when it despatched 1/9th Cav 'Pink Teams' to scour the area. Encountering a great deal of anti-aircraft fire from NVA positions, the teams duly called in numerous Marine and Air Force air strikes on large calibre AAA positions – these would have to be eliminated before any combat assault into the valley could be attempted. Alerting division headquarters to the presence of significant NVA anti-aircraft sites in the valley, the 'Pink Teams' were kept busy directing air strikes onto these positions. Once the targets had been hit, 1/9 Cav teams were again sent in to perform instant battle damage assessment in the wake of the air strikes.

Less than a week later, the first large-scale ground operation entered the A Shau Valley. The 1st Air Cav, 101st Airborne and elements of the 196th Infantry Brigade, joined by the ARVN's 1st Division and Airborne task force, moved through the valley to pre-empt enemy preparations for an attack on the Hue area, and to take advantage of the damage done by Operation *Pegasus*. The A Shau was known to be an enemy stronghold, and large numbers of men and significant quantities of freight were moving through it towards Hue. 1st Cav committed seven infantry battalions and 1/9 Cav to the operation, whilst the 196th Infantry Brigade provided three more, as did the 1st Brigade, 101st Airborne. *Delaware* became the opening counter-offensive to what became known as 'mini-Tet' – the North's spring offensive.

D/229 and 1/9 Cav were the only two Cobra units assigned to *Delaware*, and they fielded 23 helicopters between them. Each 'red' platoon in the Cavalry Troop was assigned six aircraft, although A Troop was understrength with only three AH-1s on hand. Likewise, D Company was authorised to have 12 Cobras, but only seven had been delivered at this time.

Going into the A Shau Valley, the 1st Cavalry experienced the heaviest anti-aircraft fire yet seen in South Vietnam. 'The fire that was coming up was so heavy that it sounded like a steady roar. It was a solid red wall beside me', recalled Capt Denny Miner, who participated in the initial assault into the A Shau on 19 April. AH-1G 66-15345 from D/229th was hit on numerous occasions by AK-47 fire while escorting the unit's 'slicks'. Despite the damage, the crew was able to accomplish the escort mission, although the hits in the main rotor and flight controls meant that the crew had to swap to a replacement aircraft upon returning to Camp Evans.

B Troop, 1/9 Cavalry lost its first Cobra on 28 April when it came under intense AK-47 fire while on a reconnaissance mission. With its engine having taken numerous hits and both crewmen having suffered wounds, AH-1G 66-15336 hit the ground hard. The crew nevertheless managed to escape the downed machine, which was later sling-loaded beneath a CH-47 and lifted out. Too badly damaged to be repaired in Vietnam, 66-15336 was sent back to the US to be rebuilt. It would return to combat with the 1st Cavalry Division in 1969, serving with A Battery, 2/20 Aerial Rocket Artillery (ARA) in-country until 1972.

As the lead element of the 1st Cavalry Division, 1/9 Cav took heavy casualties in the spring of 1968. May was particularly bad, with 'Alpha' Troop losing both 66-15332 and 67-15500.

On the afternoon of 3 May, CWO Bobby McKain and WO Arthur Chaney were flying AH-1G 66-15332 as half of a 'Pink Team' operating west of Khe Sanh when both helicopters began to encounter heavy 0.51-cal and 37 mm AAA. While making a pass on a 37 mm position from 1500 ft, the Cobra was struck by several rounds and the helicopter literally exploded in mid-air. Having lost its tailboom and a main rotor blade, the remains of 66-15332 then spun down to the ground on fire, the Cobra's unused ammunition detonating upon impact. Other 1st Cav aircraft in the area overflew the crash site and saw the wreckage of the AH-1 engulfed in flames, but heavy AAA prevented the recovering of the crew's remains.

361st AEROWEAPONS COMPANY

July saw the 361st Aeroweapons Company (AC) transition to the Cobra, thus becoming the first unit in II Corps to do so. Dubbed the 'Pink Panthers', the unit sent its first group of pilots and groundcrews to Bien Hoa for transition training in the first week of that month. For this, and the following two classes, 361st pilots 1Lts George Capehart and Harry Small and WO1 Barney Pultz were the Honor Graduates in their respective groups.

The unit had three platoons of four helicopters each, their old UH-1Cs being scheduled to return to Camp Holloway for inspection and maintenance and new Cobras been sent to the 'Pink Panthers' in their place. This maintained the unit's mission capability, but saw the delivery of AH-1s being slowed to a mere trickle. The 1st Platoon was finally declared operational on 31 July, and it commenced combat operations almost immediately. Armament installation, boresighting and weapons testing had restricted Cobra availability throughout July, limiting AH-1 flying time to a mere 62 hours. This was increased dramatically during August, with the unit's Cobras flying a total of 1160 combat hours.

As the 361st AWC's primary mission was armed escort, the unit was assigned convoy escort duty for the 2nd Squadron, 1st Armored Cavalry Regiment operating in the area from Pleiku to the Mang Yang Pass, along highway QL-19. A light fire team of two Cobras would cover convoys travelling the route, scouting ahead for enemy activity and reporting to

A formation of 361st AWC Cobras heads west towards the mountains of Laos, outside of their II Corps Area of Operations, in support of MACV-SOG CCC reconnaissance missions (*Mike Scheuerman/361st AWC Association*)

the convoy commander. When not directly supporting moving convoys, fire teams maintained three-minute alert status at Fire Support Base (FSB) Blackhawk, located between Pleiku and the Mang Yang Pass, offering armed assistance to friendly units in the area as needed.

The 1st Cavalry division saw its fire support capability further augmented when the 2nd Battalion, 20th Artillery (Aerial Rocket) converted to Cobras mid-month. As with other units, the conversion was a slow process until both aircraft and qualified pilots were on hand. Each of the battalion's batteries was assigned 12 Cobras, and it was calculated that these aircraft were each capable of carrying the equivalent high-explosive firepower of a battery of 105 mm howitzers. 'Blue Max', as the unit was nicknamed, became the life-saving fire support tool of 1st Cav infantrymen. By January 1969, 'Blue Max' ARA was operating all 36 of its assigned AH-1s, thus becoming the first all-Cobra unit to operate in Vietnam.

Several air cavalry units converted to the Cobra in August 1968 as well, divisional reconnaissance units from the 4th Infantry Division, D Troop, 1/10 Cav receiving its allotted nine airframes from the 334th AHC after the latter unit had received newer 1967-contract Cobras in May-June. Although these AH-1s were worn, they were nonetheless reliable. Most retained the original TAT-102A turret system, although conversion plans were underway to install the newer M-28 dual-weapon turret into these machines as they transferred to 1/10 Cav.

The M-28 turret gave the Cobra added firepower in the form of a 40 mm M-129 automatic grenade launcher mounted next to the M-134 minigun. The turret could accept one of each weapon or two of one type. Due to the scarcity of the right side grenade launcher installation hardware, dual grenade launcher configurations were rarely seen. However, dual minigun turrets became more common as the war progressed.

While D/1/10 Cav became the second Cobra unit in II Corps, other divisional reconnaissance units began converting as well. In III Corps, D Troop, 3/4th Cav (the 'Centaurs') received five new machines in August 1968, partially converting the gun platoon from the older UH-1C and giving 25th Division Reconnaissance a much-needed boost in firepower. The

WO1 Terry Queally poses in front of an A Battery, 2/20 ARA UH-1C in I Corps prior to the launch of Operation *Liberty Canyon* in late October 1968 (*Terry Queally*)

The new M-28A1 dual-weapon turret began arriving in Vietnam in mid-1968, the standard GAU-2B/A Minigun now being paired up with an M-129 40 mm grenade launcher. This improved weapons fit added significantly to the Cobra's anti-personnel capability (*Jim Moran*)

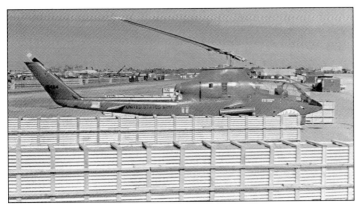

11th Armored Cavalry Regiment's Air Cav troop also converted during this time when it received nine brand new 1967-contract AH-1Gs that same month. Meanwhile, in IV Corps, D Troop, 3/5th Cavalry of the 9th Infantry Division received nine new Cobras. I Corps received a handful of new Cobras as well when F/8 Cav, attached to the AMERICAL Division (23rd Division, so named because it was raised with American and Caledonian troops during World War 2), received seven of its assigned nine AH-1Gs.

The 1st Aviation Brigade's strength was further augmented by the addition of three new Air Cavalry squadrons in II, III and IV Corps respectively. In II Corps, 7/17 Cavalry converted its three gun platoons to Cobras, as did 3/17 Cav and 7/1 Cav in III Corps.

In June 1968 7/1 Cav was reassigned from Di An to Vinh Long, in IV Corps, where the unit would stay for the remainder of the war. Following a lengthy conversion, the unit's 'Apache' Troop scored its first Cobra kills on 14 September when AH-1s from A Troop, flying in support of the 21st ARVN Division, killed nine VC and sank three sampans, one of which was carrying a large cargo of weapons, near Can Tho. A Troop Cobras also destroyed 15 enemy bunkers to complete the action. The following week, Cobras from A/7/1 Cav, again supporting ARVN ground units, engaged and eliminated a squad of VC infantry whilst patrolling in the western Mekong Delta. On 28 September 'Apache' Troop Cobras killed four VC north of Sa Dec and destroyed 21 bunkers and 14 freight-laden sampans.

While A Troop, 7/1 Cav had deployed to Vinh Long, the 'Dutchmasters' of 7/1 Cav's B Troop had remained in the Saigon area to support the 199th Light Infantry Brigade (nicknamed the 'Redcatchers') as it conducted reconnaissance-in-force operations south of the South Vietnamese capital. 28 September also saw B Troop in action when a light fire team returned anti-aircraft fire, killing two VC. In the same action, elements of 2/3 Infantry detained 24 suspects with the assistance of the 'Dutchmaster' gunships.

Elements of 7/1 Cav continued to see heavy action into October, 'Apache' Troop making heavy contact with NVA forces while supporting the 9th ARVN Infantry Division in the Mekong Delta. In the largest action, gunship crews sighted a platoon of enemy soldiers in khaki, wearing tree branches for camouflage, fording a canal north of Can Tho. The Cobras rolled in, engaging the enemy with rockets

Assigned to B/7/1 Cav's WO1 Len Constantine (aircraft commander) and SP5 Russell Stewart in the autumn of 1968, 67-15464 sits in its revetment at Vinh Long. This aircraft was heavily involved in Operation *Blackhawk* (an offensive launched in late 1968 that was designed to place round-the-clock pressure on NVA and VC infiltration routes along the Cambodian border), providing fire support for US 9th Division elements and ARVN ground units. 67-15464 was eventually destroyed on 6 March 1971 whilst on an armed reconnaissance mission during *Lam Son 719* (the invasion of Laos, which commenced on 29 January 1971) (*Russell Stewart*)

A B/7/1 Cobra departs the 'Dutchmaster' pad on a visual reconnaissance mission in late 1968. B Troop was tasked with flying both day and night sorties in order to keep a constant watch for enemy movement along the Cambodian border (*Russell Stewart*)

27

and minigun fire. After several passes, the fire team called for a ground troop insertion. 'Apache' Troop 'Blues' found 21 enemy bodies and detained three suspects.

SPECIAL OPERATIONS SUPPORT

September 1968 saw the 361st AWC commence flying support missions for Military Assistance Command Vietnam - Studies and Observations Group (MACV-SOG) reconnaissance teams that were being inserted into the tri-border region of Laos, Cambodia and Vietnam. The 361st was the first Cobra unit to be tasked with flying direct support missions outside of Vietnam. Other AH-1 units had gone across the border on certain missions, but the 361st was operating continuously in Laos and Cambodia with the reconnaissance teams of Command and Control Center (CCC).

These missions, originating out of Forward Operating Base II on the outskirts of Kontum, saw two Cobras flying in the fire team role paired up with two UH-1s from either the 57th or 119th AHC. The helicopters would head west and conduct several false insertions to confuse enemy units as to the actual team insertion point. The 361st's responsibility was to escort the 'slicks', and to provide fire support once the team was on the ground. LZ preparation was not an issue because of the stealthy nature of the reconnaissance team. Therefore, the fire team, if called upon, could instantly employ a great deal of firepower.

OPERATION *LIBERTY CANYON*

In late October, as part of Operation *Liberty Canyon*, the 1st Cavalry Division was ordered south to III Corps, where it was assigned an area of operations encompassing four provinces. According to the 1st Cav Division history, 'The equivalent of a medium-sized US town tore itself up by the roots, took wings and landed at the other end of South Vietnam. Within days, the division was conducting combat operations in III Corps, and within two weeks everything was back to normal. Supplies circulated. Paperwork flowed. And the enemy, once again, was on the run.'

Although division headquarters was at Phuoc Vinh, the division dispersed its three combat brigades to various locations around the Area of Operations (AO). This allowed greater flexibility and overlapping coverage of brigade AOs within the Divisional Tactical Area of Responsibility (TAOR).

While this split looked simple on paper, units like 1/9 Cav and 2/20 ARA were divided by troop or battery in order to fulfil responsibility to one of the three combat brigades. C Troop, 1/9 and C Battery 2/20 were assigned to 3rd Brigade and flew out of Phu Loi and Quan Loi, in western III Corps – close to the Cambodian border. The two assault helicopter battalions would provide support for the combat brigades as well, although each would be tasked according to mission specificity rather than being permanently assigned to support one brigade.

During this period, D/227 converted to the Cobra as well, taking on a dozen brand new machines after trading in its old UH-1Cs.

The final month of 1968 saw a great deal of activity taking place across the country. On 1 December, the 361st lost its first Cobra on a

B Troop, 7/1 Cavalry's SP5 Russell Stewart stands with his new charge (67-15464), which formerly served with the 334th AHC's 'Playboy' platoon – note the nose art and titling (*Russell Stewart*)

MACV-SOG CCC support mission in Attopeu province, Laos. Capt Harold Goldman and WO1 Mark Clotfelter, in AH-1G 67-15598, and Capt Gary Higgins and WO1 Norman Skipper had been tasked with covering a flight of UH-1s from the 170th AHC that were inserting a SOG Reconnaissance Team. The latter was to conduct a post-strike assessment of a B-52 raid on the Ban Tram 37 logistical command, just over the border on route 96.

Upon reaching the insertion LZ, the first 'slick', UH-1H 67-17252, was struck by numerous AK-47 rounds and crashed. Capt Goldman skillfully placed his Cobra between the enemy and the downed Huey in order to draw fire away from its occupants. A large NVA force (later determined to be of battalion strength) then began moving towards the crashed UH-1. Goldman and Clotfelter made numerous passes, keeping themselves between the enemy and the downed Huey, and expending most of their ammunition. This enabled the remaining 'slick' (callsign 'Bikini 29') to land and recover the crashed crew.

As the UH-1 was lifting off, Cobra 67-15598 received a direct hit to its engine, forcing Goldman and Clotfelter to crash land. Both men survived the impact unscathed, and Capt Goldman was able to direct Capt Higgins towards the approaching NVA in order to lay down further suppressive fire. As the UH-1 came in to pick up the downed crew, Goldman and Clotfelter added to the immense volume of suppressive fire with their own personal weapons, effectively covering the 'slick' until they were plucked to safety.

Heavy enemy activity continued throughout South Vietnam in December, with elements of the 1st Battalion, 5th Infantry engaging a company-sized force of VC approximately three miles west of Cu Chi on the 20th. The 2/12th Infantry, along with armour and gunships from the 3/4th Cavalry and B/25th Aviation, was sent to reinforce the 'Bobcats' of the 1/5th. Finally, after a seven-and-a-half-hour battle, utilising Cobras, tanks and armoured personnel carriers, the VC withdrew, unable to sustain its high level of casualties. AH-1G 67-15539 from 25th Aviation sustained minor damage during the battle when its main rotor was hit by several AK-47 rounds, although its crew was able to continue the mission. Various elements of the 25th Division counted 54 enemy dead outside their perimeter after the VC force withdrew.

OPERATION *BLACKHAWK*

While other units throughout South Vietnam were kept busy thanks to increased NVA and VC activity, 7/1 Cavalry initiated Operation *Blackhawk* in the 44th Special Tactical Zone north of Vinh Long. This offensive was designed to place round-the-clock pressure on infiltration routes along the Cambodian border, and in order for this to be achieved, all three air cavalry troops within 7/1 Cav rotated day and night assignments to keep a constant watch for enemy movement.

The troops of 7/1 employed various methods of illumination to detect movement along both water and land infiltration routes during the course of these missions, flares proving effective for night illumination. However, these devices effectively ruined the night vision of gunship pilots operating in the vicinity, leaving crews vulnerable to possible collisions with the ground as pilots recovered from their gun runs.

As if to prove this point, on one of the early night missions involving the use of flares, 'Comanche' Troop AH-1G 67-15460 nearly impacted the ground when a flare was dropped close to the gunship, blinding pilot A/C CW2 Damon Cecil. Having just managed to recover the aircraft, he then nearly collided with a spent flare canister on his pullout! The use of flares in conjunction with low level gunship operations was discontinued shortly thereafter.

A more effective method of illumination was found in the form of a Xenon searchlight, or C-123 landing light, mounted within the cabin of a UH-1H. This was employed with great success during the operation, and night-illuminated sorties were quickly dubbed 'Firefly' or 'Nighthawk' missions. The searchlight enabled targets on the ground to be lit up without blinding the Huey's Cobra gun support. While the overall target illumination was not as widespread as with the flares, the searchlight allowed specific targets to be attacked by an unseen gunship, whilst offering relative safety to the Cobra crew.

In the closing days of 1968, Operation *Blackhawk* continued to enjoy success, with 'Dutchmaster' Cobra crews reportedly killing 30 VC in an action in the U Minh forest, 25 miles north of Ca Mau, on 26 December. Nine sampans were also sunk and two enemy fortifications destroyed along the canals of the U Minh during this engagement. That same day, crews from the squadron's 'Apache' Troop claimed the destruction of 13 structures and three sampans in scattered contacts around Rach Gia, in eastern Kien Giang province.

Elsewhere in IV Corps, the 235th AWC focused on the area between Soc Trang and Phu Vinh along the Mekong Delta's Bassac River. Although not as commonly used as the Ho Chi Minh trail routes into IV Corps, the Mekong Delta provided a great deal of cover for infiltrating Communist sampans. The 235th was tasked with locating and eliminating this route, and in six separate incidents on 26 December, the unit's Cobras discovered and sunk four sampans and 52 enemy bunkers. A confirmed body count of three VC was also credited to the 'Delta Devils'.

As the year drew to a close, Cobra units had become a serious threat to the enemy in all four Corps Tactical Zones, but at a price – some 21 AH-1s had been lost to combat or accidental causes during the course of 1968.

The AH-1G had started the year as little more than an operational test aircraft, but in the space of 12 short months it had become a fully deployed, and battle-proven, combat aircraft. That said, problems were still being worked out of the helicopter's systems, and these would continue throughout the AH-1's tenure in Vietnam. Nevertheless, the Cobra and its crews had performed above all expectation in 1968. 1969 would provide even tougher challenges.

C Troop of 7/1 Cav was based at Muc Hoa for much of 1968-69, this sign marking the entrance to the co-located international airport. Note the French-Vietnamese spelling of the airfield's name (*Damon Cecil*)

C Troop, 7/1 Cavalry's CW2 Damon 'Cec' Cecil undertakes his cockpit checks prior to launching on a mission from Muc Hoa in the spring of 1969 in AH-1G 67-15460. This was Cecil's assigned Cobra for much of his tour with 'Comanche' Troop, and he flew it on numerous sorties in support of elements of the 9th Infantry Division in the Mekong Delta during Operation *Blackhawk* (*Damon Cecil*)

1969 –
PEAK STRENGTH

The New Year brought a significant increase in the number of Cobra units operating in Vietnam, and by the summer, the 1st Aviation Brigade had no fewer than 441 combat ready AH-1s – nearly 200 more were operating with divisional units throughout the country. 1969 would be a busy year for Cobra units in Vietnam, as victories and losses in the coming months would clearly illustrate.

When US infantry divisions' organic Aviation Battalions transitioned to the Cobra in late 1968 and early 1969, battalion designations, for the most part, corresponded numerically to the division in which they served. Each battalion controlled an A Company of UH-1 'slicks' and a B Company of AH-1 and UH-1C gunships. The Table of Organisation and Equipment (TO&E) for divisional gunship companies called for 12 gunships per company – six AH-1s and six UH-1Cs. By the end of January 1969, the 1st, 4th, 9th, 25th and 123rd (AMERICAL) Aviation Battalions had their full complement of gunships, and were conducting combat operations.

The 'Gambler Guns' of the 4th Aviation Battalion experienced their first Cobra action at the end of II Corps' Operation *MacArthur* in late January. The unit's presence was immediately felt when it expended over three times the ordnance used the previous month.

The 4th had created a modified version of the 'hunter-killer' team used by Cavalry squadrons, and had employed it with a great deal of success. Instead of a single OH-6 and Cobra, the 'Scorpion' 'hunter-killer' team employed two of each aircraft, increasing flexibility, firepower and the number of eyes scanning the terrain. This team often worked in conjunction with a UH-1D/H equipped with a 'people-sniffer', which could be used to detect minute amounts of ammonia in human sweat, thus locating the enemy on the ground. Once detected, the OH-6s would mark the target with CS gas grenades and then clear the area. As the CS gas deployed, the Cobras would roll in and saturate the target area with flechette rockets and 40 mm grenade fire.

Flechette rockets were new to Vietnam in 1969, having only arrived in country in the closing months of the previous year. Each rocket was similar in size to the regular 10-lb HE weapon, except for a pink nose cap which identified it as being a Flechette rocket. Inside were 1600 one-inch fin-stabilised steel nails. The flechette rocket was the ultimate anti-personnel weapon against troops caught in open areas, with a blast radius that scythed through an area approximately 300 metres in diameter. A common load for Cobras at this time were 17-lb HE rockets within the inboard XM-200/159 19-shot rocket pods and flechette rounds in the outboard XM-157/158 seven-shot

Boasting a detailed sharksmouth, this B Company, 25th Aviation Battalion, 25th Infantry Division AH-1G was nicknamed *Ghost Rider in the Sky*. The 'Diamondheads' of B/25th Aviation applied the most garish 'set of teeth' seen on Cobras in Vietnam (*Gary Schoonover*)

pods. Such a mix gave the crew the ability to select the right type of rocket for most tactical situations.

7/17 CAV's FIRST AH-1 LOSS

In mid-January C Troop, 7/17 Cavalry was conducting visual reconnaissance missions in the AO just north of Plei Djereng, west of Kontum. On the afternoon of 15 January, a 'Yellow Scarf' 'Pink Team', which was working one of the hillsides near Plei Djereng, came under intense automatic weapons fire. The team's OH-6 managed to escape without damage, but AH-1G 67-15651 was badly damaged by accurate and deadly 0.30- and 0.51-cal fire. Pilot 1Lt Sterling Cox tried to recover the aircraft after taking numerous hits, but in its rapid descent, the Cobra hit high trees and exploded. The Loach immediately radioed for the 'Blues' to be inserted to rescue any survivors. Arriving 15 minutes later, the Aero-rifle platoon, escorted by an additional Cobra fire team, quickly located the downed AH-1 and the bodies of 1Lt Cox and his front-seater, WO1 James B Petteys. During the insertion, PFC Garfield Langhorn (a Radio Telephone Operator, or RTO, with the Blue platoon) relayed orders from the C&C Huey circling overhead.

The mission was going well until both bodies were retrieved and the Blue platoon headed for the designated pick-up zone. The unit then began taking heavy automatic weapons fire from concealed bunkers ahead of them, causing several casualties. PFC Langhorn immediately called for the Cobra fire team to roll in and hit the enemy bunkers with rockets and minigun fire. Despite this support being both accurate and effective, enemy fire continued, leaving the platoon cut off and fighting for its life as darkness fell. The Cobras circling overhead expended the last of their ammunition and then headed back to base. As darkness fell, the NVA began to probe the platoon's lines. The following is an excerpt from PFC Langhorn's Medal of Honor citation.

'He then lay between the platoon leader and another man, operating the radio and providing covering fire for the wounded that had been moved to the centre of the small perimeter. Darkness soon fell, making it impossible for the gunships to give accurate support, and the aggressors began to probe the perimeter. An enemy hand grenade landed in front of Pfc Langhorn and a few feet from personnel who had become casualties. Choosing to protect these wounded, he unhesitatingly threw himself on the grenade, scooped it beneath his body and absorbed the blast.'

Langhorn died instantly. The platoon was eventually extracted at first light the following morning

January 1969 continued to be a busy month for Cobra crews across South Vietnam. The day prior to Langhorn's Medal of Honor winning engagement, a D/229th Cobra had come to the aid of a 1st Cavalry Division resupply convoy that had been ambushed south of Dau Tieng. AH-1G 67-15733 launched as a single ship relief element to assist the beleaguered convoy, the aircraft commander contacting 1st CAV immediately on take off in order to ascertain the location and size of the enemy force. When queried as to who was in charge, the radio operator informed the crew that all officers and NCOs had been killed. The helicopter commander, CW2 Dole duly let him know that he was now in command.

The surviving convoy members had taken refuge on one side of the road in a ditch, while the enemy was on the other side of the road, with the vehicles between them. The lead vehicle had been hit and was burning. The VC were shooting across the road, and under the vehicles, in an effort to pick off the American survivors. Dole advised the RTO to mark their position with smoke and then have everyone get down as low as possible as he rolled in. Dole's 'X-ray' (front seater), WO1 Ray Whitley, then placed accurate and continuous 40 mm grenade fire into the enemy ditch;

'As we flew along in broad daylight at 300 ft and 70 knots airspeed, I opened up with the grenades. I was able to walk them perfectly along the ditch. Tracers were flying by very near our bird as I did so. The enemy broke and ran. Afterward, land forces relieved the convoy. They counted 75 enemy killed in action along the ditch, and said there was evidence that many had been wounded and left blood trails as they ran or were dragged off.'

AHC TRANSITION

The gun platoons of the 114th 'Cobras' in IV Corps and 187th 'Rat Pack' in III Corps acquired the first of their assigned six AH-1s during February 1969, thus becoming the first standard Assault Helicopter Companies to be issued with the Cobra. The 'Cobras' had the honor of being the first AHC to convert to the type thanks to Bell tech reps noting the efficiency and skill with which the 114th's UH-1B gun platoon had operated some four years earlier – the 114th had been the first UH-1 unit to be deployed directly from the US to Vietnam in April 1963. Indeed, the unit had made such an impression on Bell representatives that the company's new gunship, then under construction, was named in its honour.

Both units were slow to transition, receiving both new and combat-experienced machines between February and August. Pilot transition training for standard AHCs was of low priority, and transitioning pilots to the new type suffered accordingly. Operations with mixed AH-1 and UH-1C fire teams commenced in late February, and such sorties were common during this period. These mixed formations worked well, despite the shortcomings of the older Huey. Interestingly, after these two AHCs had completed their Cobra transition in the summer of 1969, it would be nearly two years before additional Assault Helicopter Companies would acquire AH-1s in early 1971.

Two months prior to the AHCs' AH-1 conversion, the 101st Airborne Division's D Company, 101st Aviation Battalion also received its first Cobras. The first brigade of the 101st had been in-country since the summer of 1965, and it had been joined in III Corps by the remainder of the division in late 1967. Shortly after the Tet Offensive, the entire division moved northward to I Corps, around Hue. Following the arrival of its first AH-1s in December 1968, D/101 was soon augmented by three additional battalion-strength units to fill out the Airmobile Division's TO&E. The 2nd Squadron, 17th Cavalry was reorganised as an Air Cavalry squadron, and was assigned as division reconnaissance, while 4/77th ARA provided aerial fire support. The 158th Aviation Battalion arrived in-country in late February and became the division's second organic aviation battalion. By the first week of April 1969, all of these units were operational with their full complement of AH-1s.

On 6 March the 4/77th lost its first Cobra and crew. Capt John McDonnell was flying lead in a two-ship section supporting

A 'Banshee' crew chief of B/2/17 performs routine maintenance on 67-15744 at Camp Evans in the summer of 1969. Note the rotor blades sat on the steel matting in front of the AH-1G (*Vietnam Archives, Randy Kunkelman Collection*)

elements of the 101st Airborne operating in Thua Tien province. During a firing pass, McDonnell's aircraft was hit by AAA and the AH-1 disappeared into the overcast and crashed into a mountainside. The area was searched, but McDonnell could not be located. His pilot, Lt Ronald Greenfield, was found and medically evacuated aboard a 2/17 Cav OH-6.

Eleven days later, the 1st Infantry Division and the 11th Armored Cavalry Division caught a large contingent of bicycle-mounted NVA troops in the open in the Michelin Rubber Plantation in III Corps. The rapid response of these units initiated Operation *Atlas Wedge* to eliminate this threat. It was soon determined that this contingent of NVA was a scouting element for the 7th NVA Division. Led by Lt Col Bill Haponski's 1st Squadron, 4th Cav, the units moved into the plantation on 18 March.

Control of D Troop (callsign 'Darkhorse'), which was Lt Col Haponski's air cav element, was unclear at this point. While technically under his command, division headquarters had taken the troop under operational control at the beginning of *Atlas Wedge*. However, the unit was partially returned to Haponski two days later.

Returning to 18 March, at 1615 hrs one of the 'Darkhorse' 'hunter-killer' team scouts came under automatic weapons fire from several locations. The Cobra rolled in, firing several pairs of rockets and the minigun and grenade launcher. The team claimed five probable KBA, but was unable to confirm a body count.

At dusk on the 21st, C Troop (armoured cavalry) made contact with enemy troops and engaged, calling for gunship support. First on the

This 11th ACR 'Thunderhorse' Cobra was photographed escorting 'sniffer' UH-1s, with troop detecting sensors aboard, on an Operation *Atlas Wedge* mission over the Michelin Rubber Plantation in March 1969. *Atlas Wedge* was hastily launched after the 1st Infantry Division and the 11th Armored Cavalry Division caught a large contingent of bicycle-mounted NVA troops in the open in the plantation. 11th ACR AH-1Gs flew closely in support of both divisions, and helped to eliminate this large enemy force (*John Baumhackl*)

An M-113 APC of the 11th ACR idles alongside Cobras of C battery, 2/20 ARA near the Michelin Rubber Plantation in March 1969. AH-1G crews regularly operated in conjunction with the ubiquitous APC throughout the Vietnam conflict (*Jim Moran*)

Marked with the US Cavalry's distinctive crossed sabres on its nose, this AH-1G of D/3/4 Cav idles in a clearing, under the watchful gaze of an M-48 tank crew, whilst on a sortie in III Corps (*Author's collection*)

scene was an AH-1 fire team led by 'Darkhorse 38', who called for C Troop to mark its position with smoke. The Cobra then attacked. The team was on station for ten minutes, and had expended all of its ammunition by the time it was relieved by another 'Darkhorse' fire team. This second formation duly reported encountering heavy auto-weapons fire from the east. Once the second 'Darkhorse' fire team had expended its ammunition, a Cobra fire team from B Company, 1st Aviation Battalion, relieved them.

The platoon commander, in 'Rebel 36', led this third fire team, and reported to Lt Col Haponski that approximately two squads of enemy infantry had been spotted armed with automatic weapons and rocket-propelled grenades (RPGs). One of C Troop's APCs was hit by an RPG at this time. 'Rebel 36' and his wingman continued to make firing passes until they were out of ammunition. Lt Col Haponski related in his daily journal that 'Dark fell, and the gunships I called in made red streams of light come from the sky as they sprayed the area only a few metres ahead of us with their miniguns and rockets'.

By 2015 hrs a 'Spooky' AC-47 gunship had arrived on station overhead, replacing the rotating Cobra fire teams that had expended their ordnance. 'Spooky' then remained on station until 2200 hrs, when contact was broken. C Troop initially reported no body count, but would conduct a sweep at first light to confirm.

Cobras from D/1/4, B/1, Air/11 and 2/20 ARA were instrumental in this engagement, and numerous others flown during *Atlas Wedge*. For example, during the defence of FSB Doc in the early morning of 23 March, 'Firefly' teams of two Cobras and a searchlight equipped Huey, coupled with 'Spooky' gunships, continually kept fire on the perimeter of the base. Cobras were instructed to expend their ordnance 1000 metres north of the base to silence sporadic mortar fire. Both 'Blue Max' and 'Darkhorse' fire teams remained on station throughout the night, placing accurate fire where directed from Doc.

The heaviest fighting of *Atlas Wedge* occurred on 30 March when Task Force 'Haponski' attacked a full strength NVA battalion discovered in the Michelin plantation. 'Darkhorse' and 'Rebels' Cobras were active throughout the day and into the night supporting the attack. Total US casualties for the operation were 22 killed in action and 100 wounded. The operation continued through to 1 April, netting 421 known enemy killed, over six tons of rice, 120 personal weapons, four crew-served weapons and many tons of documents and equipment.

NEW EQUIPMENT

During the spring of 1969, helicopter pilots and crews in Vietnam began to receive new equipment designed to increase survivability. The Nomex fire-retardant two-piece flight suit was standardised at this time, allowing the earlier cotton K-2B to be withdrawn from service. The APH-5 standard flight helmet, which offered no ballistic protection for aircrews, was also replaced by the AFH-1 ballistic protective helmet. The latter was a particularly welcome addition, as AAA had dramatically increased in 1968. Finally, helicopter flight crews received one piece of equipment that would save numerous lives throughout the remainder of the war. The Aircrew Body Armour, or 'Chickenplate', as it became known, was a bulletproof vest with removable ceramic/fibreglass plates capable of stopping a 0.30-cal bullet. A front and back plate could be carried for crew chiefs and gunners, while pilots, because of their armoured seats, only needed the front plate.

APACHE SNOW

One month after *Atlas Wedge* had come to an end, another major US operation began to the north in I Corps – *Apache Snow*. 'Pink Teams' of the 2/17th Cavalry were scouting the western approaches of the A Shau Valley around Ap Bia Mountain (also known as Hill 937) when they discovered numerous NVA bunkers. On 10 May, the 3rd Battalion, 187th Infantry combat assaulted into the A Shau Valley and made contact with the enemy after 4/77th AH-1s had prepped five designated LZs with over 400 17-lb HE rockets. According to the C Battery unit history, contact was made at two of the five locations, and resulted in a number of enemy soldiers being killed in action. Documents captured at these locations revealed the presence of the 29th NVA Regiment.

Combat was not limited to Hill 937, however. A forward operating base was established at FSB Currahee to support the ARA and 2/17th Cavalry with fuel and armament. C Battery was the first to maintain a 'hot' section of Cobras on station at Currahee to respond to urgent close air support missions. Shortly after the refuel/rearm point was established, it was attacked in force by NVA infantry and sappers, destroying 3000 gallons of JP4 and 11,000 rockets. The clean up took several days, but did not severely affect 4/77th operations in support of ground elements of the 101st

WO1 Dave 'Babysan' Fuller of A Battery, 4/77th ARA loads a personalised 10-lb rocket into an XM-159 19-shot pod affixed to the outer hardpoint of his Cobra's left stub wing (*Dave Fuller*)

Airborne. Eventually, the entire battalion operated out of Currahee on a round the clock basis.

Bravo Company of the 187th made heavy contact with NVA late the next day, and Lt Honeycutt responded quickly by directing the 'Griffins' of C Battery, 4/77 ARA to support his attack. Through the 'fog of war', a section of ARA Cobras misfired their initial rocket volley and two rounds hit Lt Honeycutt's command post (CP), wounding him and 34 others and killing two. This incident ceased effective command and control of the 187th's attack, forcing the battalion to dig in for the night and regroup. Honeycutt then demanded that all aircraft check with his CP before launching strikes, and he halted all ARA support until friendly positions were marked more clearly.

American tactics at this time focused on the massive application of high explosives, mainly from the air, to accomplish mission objectives. The AH-1G was the ideal platform for putting large amounts of ordnance on-target within metres of friendly forces. The employment of such awesome firepower was effective under most circumstances, but as with Lt Honeycutt's CP, was considerably less effective when operating over triple-canopy jungle. Helicopter gunships created massive enemy casualties and limited the NVA's ability to mass for counterattacks, but LZ preparatory fires seldom eliminated communist positions. The dense jungle and the mountainous terrain protected the enemy from rocket and grenade fragments, as did their well-prepared defences.

The 4/77th provided excellent fire support throughout the engagement, despite the early setbacks. In the opening days of the battle for what became known as 'Hamburger Hill', C Battery fired 4400 rockets, destroyed 12 bunkers and had a confirmed body count of 19 KBA. On 12 May, WOs Carl Rajotte and Richard Freeman were recommended for the Air Medal with V device for their actions in support of 3/187th Infantry in the face of continuous 0.51-cal anti-aircraft fire, flying repeated missions until the enemy was silenced.

On 14 May, an unusual incident occurred to an A Troop, 2/17th 'Pink Team', as Len Constantine, aircraft commander of AH-1G 67-15698, relates;

'I suspect encounters between aircraft south of the DMZ were rare. An encounter between an AH-1G and a MiG-21 might qualify as unique. We were working the eastern slope of Ap Bia Mountain, in the A Shau Valley, when the call "Bandit" came up on "Guard" (the standard emergency radio frequency common to all military aircraft). It could have been an Air Force C-121 with the MiG on radar. I never knew.

'Looking around, there was a fast mover in the distance flying up the long axis of the A Shau from the south. He wasn't making

An aerial shot of the ancient citadel in the city of Hue. 101st Airborne operations in the A Shau Valley in early 1969 prevented NVA units from advancing on the former Vietnamese capital, thus foiling communist plans for capturing the city (*Jack Hepler*)

any smoke and his wings just didn't look like one of ours. I made a call to the Loach to come up out of the bushes. I couldn't cover him down in the weeds and protect him from the oncoming threat as well.

'The head-on profile of the MiG-21 was obvious, and closing very quickly. I didn't have the speed to run in a Cobra, so I just armed my turret, raised the nose and my gunner pressed the trigger. A GAU-2B at high rate puts out 4000 rounds of 7.62 mm a minute. By the time he passed us, we'd given him a few seconds worth. Although he had to have taken some hits, I was surprised that the MiG pilot did not alter his course. He literally roared right over me in a straight line, headed most likely for the MiG base at Vinh. As the 7.62 mm had little effect, I snapped around about the axis of the rotor and fired half a dozen pair of 2.75 FFAR after him. For an instant, I thought that I had him. Two rockets arced up at him and literally passed just above his canopy. This finally elicited a response. The MiG's wings bobbled nervously and the afterburner lit. I sat there in my seat transfixed as the MiG-21 climbed away, and out of my grasp.

'Then the thought slammed into me – I had no idea where his wing-man might be! High, slow and helpless, I was the dumbest "Warrant" in the world, and was certainly going to die immediately for this tactical faux pas. However, the cannon fire never came. I transmitted a spot report and we returned to our more mundane existence of Air Cav pilots. The MiG was probably alone, most likely on a recce flight.

'When we got back to Camp Eagle that evening, there was a crowd to meet us. They eagerly wanted to hear about the thrilling dogfight. They had heard that we had killed a MiG! I could only explain, sheepishly, that I had missed him, and that today was not the beginning of my career as an ace.'

On 15 May the 1st Brigade of the 101st Airborne was detached and sent south to assist elements of the AMERICAL Division that had been strained by a major NVA assault throughout its TAOR. This quick reaction operation was named Operation *Lamar Plain/Nathan Hale* and AH-1 sorties focused on B Troop, 2/17 Cav and B Battery 4/77, ARA.

AMERICAL Cobra units (F/8th Cav, D/1/1 Cav and B/123rd Avn) were stretched to their utmost, covering the largest TAOR in Vietnam with a relatively small number of gunships. On 18 May a D/1/1 heavy 'Pink Team' engaged an NVA unit equipped with 0.51-cal machine guns. The team launched at around 0830 hrs and headed west out of Tam Ky. There were numerous signs of enemy activity in the area, but no NVA troops. The Loach then moved in down low along a west-east ridgeline and began taking fire. Capt Mike Henry, in AH-1G 67-15686 'DDAP' ('Dead Dinks Are Pacified' – a satirical commentary by GIs on the post-1968 'pacification' programme initiated in South Vietnam by Military Assistance Command Vietnam) 'Sword 75', rolled in, but his weapons failed to fire. After resetting the guns, they functioned properly, and Henry initiated his second pass on the NVA positions. As he pulled the AH-1 up, he was hit by 0.51-cal fire;

'Even the infantry called "'Sword 75', you're taking hits!" I said "Roger that" in a sort of cocky manner – I'd been in country about ten months then, and had taken lots of fire. Well, suddenly the front

These detail photographs reveal the extent of the damage inflicted on the cockpit of D/1/1 Cav's AH-1G 67-15686 *DDAP* after it had been hit by several 0.51-cal rounds whilst flying a reconnaissance sweep near Chu Lai on 16 May 1969. Although gunner Capt Leo Huber was killed and aircraft commander Capt Mike Henry wounded in the left leg and right hand, the AH-1G stayed aloft, allowing the pilot to keep the helicopter under control and perform a running landing back at Tam Ky. At the lower left of the photograph showing the control panel is the top of the severed cyclic (*Robert Wiggins*)

canopy exploded with a big bang, and I recall another big bang behind my seat. Another hit took out the FM radio and the top of the cyclic. This was how I got the wounds to my left leg and right hand. My pinky finger was hit and that would hurt for a long time.

'I yelled at Leo to take control of the helicopter because I didn't have a cyclic, but when I looked toward the front, I could see he was most likely dead already. His body was smashed into what remained of the front cockpit and there was blood all over.

'The ship started a right roll. I reached down and found just a few inches of the cyclic sticking out of the floor. I started an auto-rotation, but noticed the 0.51-cal fire crossing over and around the AH-1, so I ruled out landing in the middle of the bad guys. The engine was still running, so I flew it back to Tam Ky and did a running landing on the runway because I didn't know how badly the helicopter was damaged.'

These engagements were the opening volley of the NVA's summer offensive that would continue through to August 1969. 101st Airborne and AMERICAL Cobra units would fly round the clock missions for the next several months

WITHDRAWAL BEGINS

With President Richard Nixon's announcement of the American pullout on 8 June 1969, the 9th Infantry Division was slated to return to the US by the end of the summer. The 9th Aviation Battalion began winding down operations shortly after the announcement. Although only in existence as a Cobra unit for six months, the 'Stingrays' of B Company had been essential in the support of 9th Division ground assets since the unit's arrival in 1967.

The 'Stingrays', under Capt Robert Schultz, had been one of the few gunship companies to work in conjunction with the Mobile Riverine Force operating in IV Corps. This air/waterborne assault group was extremely effective in hunting VC/NVA sampans in the Mekong Delta. After converting to the Cobra, the unit had acquitted itself admirably in the various actions of late December 1968 around Dong Tam.

AH-1G 67-15815 *HAPPINESS IS A WARM GUN* of the B/9th Avn Bn was flown from Dong Tam and Phu Loi by Capt Robert Schultz in early 1969. Operating as 'Stingray 6', this machine was brand new when delivered to the unit (*Author's collection*)

As the 9th wound down operations, its aircraft were issued piecemeal to various units around South Vietnam. Of the five Cobras the company had on hand in August, two went to units of the 1st Cavalry Division as replacement aircraft – one to B Troop, 3/17th Cav at Di An and one to A Troop, 7/17th Cav in II Corps. D/3/5 Cav, which functioned as part of the 9th Aviation Battalion, would stay on in Vietnam after the division had left, absorbing the remaining Cobra as attrition replacements.

The winding down of the 9th Division was the first in a series of phased withdrawals designed to incrementally de-escalate the American side of the war, while increasing ARVN involvement. Vietnamization, as it was called, removed the main US ground combat formations from Vietnam, but as with the case of D/3/5 Cav, and numerous units later on, air assets were apparently exempt from this withdrawal until the very end.

NVA SUMMER OFFENSIVE

The North Vietnamese assault towards Chu Lai in mid-May 1969 was the beginning of a series of offensives designed to cut South Vietnam in half. American combat units were heavily engaged throughout June and July, calling on Cobras for fire support across I Corps.

By August it was clear that the enemy was making a major push through the Hiep Duc Valley – the border between Quang Nam and Quang Tin provinces. Units of the 1st Marine Division were operating north of the valley out of Da Nang, while the AMERICAL Division was to the south, based at Chu Lai. Elements of both units had made contact with NVA formations by the middle of the month, engaging in a series of firefights. The 2nd NVA Division had moved into the valley in force, but had for the most part eluded contact.

On 18 August, Bravo Company, 4/31 Infantry made contact in the village at the base of Nui Chum Mountain. Within minutes the company had been surrounded, and suffered seven fatalities. Capt Gayle called for gunship support and received the reply that 'Blue Ghost' Cobras were already en route. Arriving overhead, the AH-1 crews had the infantrymen pop smoke to identify their lines. 'Blue Ghost' lead came in low and his gunner concentrated 40 mm fire just outside of

Pilots of F Troop, 8th Cavalry 'Blue Ghosts' rest between missions at Tien Phuoc during the height of the NVA Summer Offensive in 1969 (*Robert Wiggins*)

Maintenance is carried out on an F Troop Cobra at Tien Phuoc. The Troop's 'Blue Ghost' emblem is clearly visible on the AH-1G's 'doghouse' access door (*Robert Wiggins*)

the American perimeter, resulting in a number of NVA kills, and forcing a squad of enemy troops to retreat. The communist soldiers were well camouflaged, but constant 40 mm and minigun fire from the Cobras broke the enemy attack and took some pressure off the American infantry.

At dusk, 'Blue Ghost' Cobras escorted a Medevac Huey in to extract Bravo Company's wounded, the AH-1s providing cover fire by shooting up the hedgerows along Bravo Company's perimeter. However, one 0.51-cal machine gun opened up and hit the Medevac several times, partially severing its tail rotor drive shaft. The UH-1H pulled out at a precarious angle, but returned to base empty. An hour later another Medevac was attempted, this time successfully.

'Blue Ghost' Cobras were instrumental in saving Bravo Company, 4/31, providing constant close air support for both Army and Marine units in the valley. Lt Col Marvin Lugger's 2nd Battalion, 7th Marines moved out on the morning of 25 August and made immediate contact with the two enemy regiments. F Company came under intense mortar, RPG and automatic weapons fire, as did Lugger's command group in the centre. Lugger called in air strikes – both 'fast movers' and helicopters – and napalm was dropped within 50 metres of friendly units. Companies G and H were still heavily engaged on the right flank, and Company F was pinned down and unable to move on the left. Lugger requested his reserve company to reinforce his weakened left flank, and at dusk Echo Company was combat assaulted into the AO, and F Company, no longer combat effective, was pulled out under cover of the guns of the 'Blue Ghosts'.

By the end of August, the 2nd NVA Division had ceased to exist as a combat formation. Close support by 'Blue Ghost' AH-1s had decimated communist ranks, and saved US ground units on several occasions.

MORTAR ATTACK

1st Cavalry Division Cobras were busy through the late summer and into the early autumn of 1969. 5 September brought a crippling blow to the 'Smiling Tigers' at Daub Ting, when their base was attacked in the early hours of the morning by a VC mortar team which had got within range of the flightline. Numerous shells were lobbed onto the airfield, and the mortar patrol fire team was immediately directed toward the enemy fire, but not before six of the 'Smiling Tigers' Cobras had been damaged by enemy fire. AH-1G 66-15260 and 66-15345 were damaged so severely that they were sent to a rear maintenance depot for rebuilding – neither would return to the unit. Groundcrews, working around the clock, repaired the remaining four damaged Cobras.

This unique in-flight photograph was taken by WO1 Jim Moran from the aircraft commander's seat, the camera lens looking through the M-73 illuminated gunsight (*Jim Moran*)

7/17th Cav was also heavily committed to combat in the final months of 1969. On 2 November AH-1G 67-15616 was part of a 'Scorpion' reconnaissance team operating approximately eight miles south of Duc Lap, near the old Firebase Helen. At around 1600 hrs the OH-6 flown by WO1 Nowicki spotted three foxholes along highway QL14. The Loach began taking AK-47 fire and Nowicki was hit in the foot and the helicopter's radio system was destroyed. As soon as the OH-6 received fire, its crew withdrew east, allowing the Cobras to roll in. The damaged helicopter touched down roughly five miles away and the second Loach moved in to assist. Nowicki and his observer, Lt Curran, climbed aboard, but as WO1 Grega pulled pitch, the OH-6 came under intense 0.51-cal fire and crashed.

Moments later WO1 Michael Peterson, who was the aircraft commander of the second Cobra, arrived overhead;

'I was circling the area, and had half expended my ordnance, when I noticed someone climb out of the burning LOH and stagger up the hill in a daze, falling and getting up. I descended a little lower, and I could see that his arms, face and neck were burned. He was not wearing a Nomex shirt – I later learned from him that it had been burned off. To my knowledge there were no other "slicks" in the area, so I elected to go in and see if I could pick him up on my ammo bay doors. I made two passes, and on the second I was struck in the leg and foot.'

The Cobra began taking both 0.30- and 0.51-cal hits, one of the latter hitting the cyclic and tearing it in half. Peterson continued;

'I lost control of the helicopter as a result of losing the cyclic, and we descended into the side of the hill and the rotor blades contacted the ground and we flipped over, causing us to land inverted. I quickly released both myself and Capt Luis Chirichigno, who was in the front seat. I ran up there and pulled him out and dragged him over to George Grega – the man I had attempted to rescue. We lay in the field for approximately two-and-a-half hours, during which time both WO1 Grega and Chirichigno passed out.

'They were both in pretty bad shape, so I elected to try to flag down a helicopter in another open field about 200 metres to the south of us, thinking it might have been a little more secure. The remaining Cobra rolled in and expended its ordnance on the area, and its pilot then seemed to indicate a pick up point. After dark, a Huey came in and picked up Lt Curran, but drew fire before the remaining crewmen could reach the "slick". During the night WO1 Grega died of his wounds.'

The remaining Cobra and Loach crewmen – Chirichigno, Peterson and Nowicki – attempted to escape and evade, and did so for the next three days. Chirichigno was the most seriously wounded, and was moaning a great deal, and VC infantry eventually captured the group on the afternoon of 6 November. Nowicki and Peterson were released a month later, but Capt Chirichigno was taken to North Vietnam and eventually released in March 1973.

NEW WEAPONS

The most serious threat to the Cobra was the increasing presence of communist 0.51-cal heavy machine guns in South Vietnam. There was little a helicopter could do against such a weapon except get away from it, or get in close enough to kill the gun. The Army began introducing the new XM-35 weapons system in mid-December 1969, and results were almost immediate. The system consisted of a cut-down 20 mm M-61 Vulcan cannon (known as the M-195) de-rated to fire 750 rpm, two ammunition canisters fitted over the skids, holding a total of 950 rounds, and the associated crossover ammunition feed chutes. The flat trajectory and long range of the new weapon finally gave Cobra crews the ability to stand-off outside 0.51-cal range and eliminate AAA positions.

Early fielding of the system produced favourable results, but a redesign of some of the helicopter's systems was necessary. According to Capt Hugh Mills;

'Usually, the blast of the gun knocked the Stability Control and Augmentation System (SCAS) offline, and you could flip inverted if your dive was over 70 degrees and at speeds in excess of 160 knots. If not, the intervalometer cycled and your rockets fired. The front seater also had to hold his canopy handle closed or the blast would cause it to vibrate open, allowing the canopy to be torn off. Ammunition carried was High Explosive Incendiary (HEI), and Target Practice Tracer (TPT), spaced five rounds apart. The AH-1s were fitted with fibreglass blast panels on the side of the fuselage to stop the muzzle blast from punching holes in the skin. Still, it was perfectly normal to punch off SCAS, have the front seater grab the handle and turn the weapons arm switch to safe (the XM-35 had a separate panel from the other weapons located in the middle and bottom of the Aircraft Commander's panel) as one rolled in.'

Another 'special' weapon beginning to appear in late 1969 was the CS rocket. Only cleared for certain operations, and not when friendly units were in the area, the CS rocket gave Cobra crews a decisive edge when attacking bunker complexes. The CS gas in the rockets would get NVA infantry out of their bunkers and into the open, where flechette rockets could then be employed with devastating effect. In the late spring of 1970, these weapons would undergo their first major combat test.

The XM-35 weapon system was introduced to operations in Vietnam in late 1969, with suitably modified AH-1Gs being evenly split between I and IV Corps. The cut-down 20 mm M-61 Vulcan cannon (known as the M-195 when fitted to the Cobra) was de-rated to fire 750 rpm, with ammunition fed via two canisters attached to either side of the fuselage above the skids. Each of these held 950 rounds, as well as the associated crossover ammunition feed chutes. The flat trajectory and long range of the M-195 at last gave Cobra crews a chance to duel with the NVA's 0.51-cal AAA positions, whilst at the same time remaining out of range of the previously deadly heavy machine gun. Outboard of the cannon can be seen a XM-157 seven-shot rocket pod (*Jim Moran*)

Fresh off the Bell Helicopter production line, this newly arrived 1967-contract AH-1G awaits the fitment of its turret weapons and assignment to an operational unit (*Author's collection*)

1970 – UNLEASHED INTO CAMBODIA

The successes of *Apache Snow* in May 1969 led the 101st Airborne south to Thua Thien province, near Hue, in support of Operation *Randolph Glen* in late 1969. This offensive, which was conducted in conjunction with the ARVN's 1st Infantry Division, was to provide a shield to the populated areas of the province against NVA infiltration. ARA Cobras were kept busy throughout the operation, flying in support of both divisions.

In the late morning of 31 January 1970, 4/77 ARA and D/158 AHB supported a major attack by the 1st ARVN division in the foothills of Thua Thien Province. A section from the 'Dragons' of A Battery was first on the scene, and through careful coordination with the ARVN ground commander and an Air Force O-2A FAC aircraft, they provided devastating fire support for the troops on the ground. Due to previous airstrikes and defoliation operations in the area, very little vegetation remained, and bunkers were clearly visible from the air.

Once the 'Dragon' section had expended their loads, a section from the 'Redskins' of D/158 AHB took up their station and continued placing fire on the enemy bunker line. While the 'Redskins' were on station, 'Griffins' Cobras from C/4/77 also arrived in the area and were briefed in the air by the departing 'Dragon' section and the ground commander. Due to the closeness of the fighting, the ARVN commander would not permit the use of turret weapons – a rather odd request, considering the minigun was considerably more precise than rockets.

As the 'Redskins' departed to refuel and rearm, the 'Griffins' section, led by WO1 Stephen Scheidling, located the friendly positions and called for the FAC to mark the target. Scheidling and his wingman rolled in, and each fired their rockets on the bunker line. As they were making their firing pass, one of the Cobra pilots spotted an unknown unit on an adjacent hill. The ARVN ground commander confirmed that these troops were hostile and gave the crew permission to engage them with turret weapons. The section took heavy return fire while completing their passes over the enemy unit, but exacted a heavy toll on the exposed troops. Upon expending the last of their ammunition, the section was relieved by two more 'Griffins' AH-1s, led by Capt James Barnett.

The 'Griffins' remained on station all afternoon, providing fire support for the advancing ARVN units and covering them as they reached the NVA positions. Once ARVN forces had achieved their objectives, 'Griffins' Cobras escorted in three 'slicks' of Hueys to recover the South Vietnamese wounded and take 14 PoWs and captured documents to the rear for interrogation and processing. Two more

'Dustoff' missions were covered in the waning daylight hours, and 'Griffins' Cobras also remained on station to cover ARVN troops cleaning up the last remnants of resistance on the hill.

In all, ARA aircraft contributed to 60 enemy killed in action, 14 captured and the seizure of significant quantities of weapons and documentation. Thanks to the tenacity of the 'Griffins'' effort, not a single ARVN soldier had been lost during the operation.

IV CORPS OPERATIONS – FEBRUARY & MARCH

The 'Silver Spurs' of A/3/17 Cavalry departed their base at Di An at the end of 1969 and moved south to reinforce IV Corps. 'Silver Spur' 'hunter-killer' teams operated throughout the Ca Mau peninsula, seeking out and engaging small NVA units. CW2 Dave Tela recalls one particular mission;

'It was an unusual day since an Army general, flying in the command and control helicopter, was monitoring us. A couple of "hunter-killer" teams were at this particular location outside of Kien Long, since we were preparing for a ground troop insertion. It was an overcast, hazy day. It became readily apparent that the enemy had located itself in the immediate area where the insertion was to take place. This was kind of spooky, for it was obvious that there had been an intelligence leak prior to the mission – I had not experienced this before.'

The enemy fire intensified significantly, and it became clear that Tela's team had not stumbled upon a small unit, but rather a large NVA formation that was deliberately positioned to counter the impending combat assault. Upon entering the area, Tela's scout immediately spotted a group of well-equipped enemy soldiers, so he began to climb out of range of the enemy weapons. Reacting to protect the Loach, Tela fired several pairs of rockets at the enemy positions and covered the scout in its flight to safety.

'There was so much action that even the command and control aircraft had its door gunners firing into the area. It was totally unexpected, and clearly revealed the real cost of intelligence leaks, however they happened. The one thing that sticks out in my mind is that I thought I would catch hell for flying too close and too low to the action.'

Working in conjunction with other 'Silver Spur' Cobras, Tela descended to low level to accurately place fire on any positions that might threaten friendly aircraft. Skillfully manoeuvring, Tela remained on call so as to be able to place suppressive fire under the other aircraft, yet he was evasive

AH-1G 69-16439 awaits its next mission at Tay Ninh, in western III Corps. Flown by three-time DFC-recipient Dave Tela on his medal winning mission of 16 February 1970, this aircraft was a 20 mm cannon-modified Cobra that went on to see extensive combat in Cambodia in May-June of that same year. It was reassigned to C/2/17 Cav in June 1971 and then F/4 Cav in early 1972, before finally returning to the US after the ceasefire. Configured as a 'super scout', 69-16439 carried three XM-157 seven-shot rocket pods and turret weapons, as well as the 20 mm cannon (*Dave Tela*)

CW2 Dave Tela receives his DFC from his commanding officer just days after flying his 16 February mission (*Dave Tela*)

enough to prevent the enemy gunners from hitting his Cobra. As the command and control aircraft ceased firing, Tela began placing devastating aerial rocket fire into the enemy, repeatedly making low passes over the NVA positions and assisting in the destruction of several enemy anti-aircraft guns. CW2 Tela's actions enabled the combat assault to succeed, and saved the lives of numerous Allied infantrymen. Dave Tela was awarded the Distinguished Flying Cross (DFC) for his actions on 16 February.

Mission tempo had increased in both III and IV Corps towards the end of 1969, and it remained high through the spring and early summer of 1970. In March, for example, the 235th, A/3/17 and 7/1 had all been flying round the clock missions in IV Corps. During this time, one of the most unique 'shootdowns' of any type of aircraft in Vietnam happened to a Cobra from 1st Platoon, 235th AWC.

Column cover was usually a tedious and dull mission which saw AH-1 crews running a racetrack pattern over a vehicle column, acting as a 'super scout' to determine if the road ahead was clear. On 3 March WO1 Roscoe Armstrong, callsign 'Satan 10', was leading a heavy fire team at low level, escorting a fuel convoy from Ca Mau to 'Rockjaw' in IV Corps. After several low level orbits, with nothing spotted, it appeared to be a routine mission. As Armstrong's Cobra (AH-1G 68-15210) passed over the convoy's lead jeep at an altitude of roughly 50 ft, there was an immense explosion and the helicopter began a rapid descent. Armstrong, unaware of what had just happened, was able to maintain enough control to set the stricken Cobra down on the side of the road. He called over the intercom to check his front-seater's status and received no reply. Apparently, flying glass from the canopy had severed his gunner's intercom line, making communication impossible.

Quickly exiting the stricken Cobra, both crewmen soon realised what had brought them down. As they passed over it, the lead jeep hit a booby-trapped 105 mm artillery round and the resultant explosion destroyed both the vehicle and Armstrong's brand new Cobra! Miraculously, none of the men in the jeep were killed. Both pilots suffered minor cuts and bruises, but were flying again a few days later.

The US withdrawal sped up in 1970. In April, the 1st Infantry Division was sent home, while the core of its aviation assets remained in-country. The 'Rebels' of B Company, 1st Aviation Battalion were combined with the 'Darkhorse' Troop, 1/4th Cavalry to form C Troop, 16th Cavalry, which retained the callsign 'Darkhorse'. C Troop moved south to Can Tho and set up operations there in the early summer months of 1970.

Towards the end of 1969 and into early 1970, American units in the southern two Corps areas had experienced increasing frustration with the rules of engagement in respect to combating the enemy in Cambodia. Although it was widely known that NVA and VC units operated along the Ho Chi Minh trail just over the border, US units were powerless to do anything. Officially, Cambodia was neutral, and therefore off limits to US combat units. However, the NVA had expanded the trail and established numerous enclaves in northeastern Cambodia that served as jumping off points for the continued infiltration of South Vietnam.

Right and below
AH-1G 68-15210 was downed in one of the more unusual VC attacks of the war. WO1 Roscoe Armstrong was providing gun cover for a IV Corps convoy when he flew over the lead jeep at low level just as the vehicle hit a booby-trapped 105 mm artillery shell. The jeep was destroyed, and debris from the explosion shot into the sky, wrecking Armstrong's Cobra in the process. Although severely damaged, the helicopter was ultimately rebuilt and returned to combat the following year. Miraculously, no one was killed in this freakish incident (*Roscoe Armstrong*)

Paul Garrity (left), Newkirk (right) and a third unidentified C/2/20 pilot 'chew the fat' between missions at Quan Loi in mid-1970 (*Jim Moran*)

Despite being officially forbidden, Cobras began flying into Cambodian airspace in late 1969 to reconnoitre areas where there was 'no suspected enemy activity'. Heavy AAA invariably greeted these flights. By the spring of 1970, these sorties had become routine. CW2 Paul Garrity of C Battery, 2/20 ARA remembers;

'We had a section on two minute alert, 24 hours a day, so when you got a mission, you didn't know where you were going. For Cambodia before May 1970, you would have a mission inside of Vietnam, and then when you got there you were told to call a certain frequency. Someone would then give you a mission to other coordinates from there. Well, after a while you knew once the grid references had come through exactly where you were going. "Oh shit" was a typical response from us in the helicopter, because we were all aware that if anything happened to us over the border before May 1970 it was "our fault". Officially, we would have to claim that we were off course or had got lost, when in reality we had been ordered into Cambodian airspace.

'These sorties were performed for Special Forces teams over the border, so you were firing in support of a small groups – maybe three to five men on the ground – and most of the time they would be whispering to you because the enemy was right there with them.'

UNLEASHED – THE CAMBODIAN INVASION

As the first major operation of Vietnamization, ARVN units began the initial push into Cambodia on 29 April 1970 through the 'Parrot's Beak' and 'Angel's Wing' areas of III Corps. The following day, US ground and air units initiated their assault into Cambodia from both southern Corps areas on a broad front. Three major US combat units crossed the border in the early morning of 1 May, the task force being built around the 1st Cavalry Division, with the 25th Division on its southern flank, the 11th Armored Cavalry regiment to the north and elements of the 1st Aviation Brigade in direct aerial support.

The initial thrusts caught the NVA almost completely off guard, with 'Pink Teams' of 1/9 Cavalry strafing and rocketing numerous trucks in the open along the Ho Chi Minh trail almost at their leisure. The surprise was so complete that many NVA units broke and ran in utter confusion and terror. In the northern sector,

Two C Battery Cobras (67-15600 and an unidentified machine) sit idling at Bu Dop prior to heading west into Cambodia (*Jim Moran*)

'Thunderhorse' Cobras from the Air Cav troop of the 11th Armored Cavalry regiment provided air cover for the regiment's tanks and APCs as they sped towards Snoul after pushing through the heavy resistance thrown up by the 7th NVA Division.

LZs were prepped early in the day by B-52 strikes, as well as artillery from II Field Force, which fired over 5000 rounds of HE. Cobras from 'Blue Max' 2/20 ARA continued pre-assault LZ preparation by firing hundreds of high explosive and flechette rounds into intended LZs before the 'slicks' arrived on the scene. 'Blue Max' AH-1s remained overhead and continued to place accurate rocket, minigun and grenade fire into the treeline, killing numerous NVA troops and keeping the pressure on so as to allow the 5th ARVN Airborne Battalion to conduct a virtually unopposed combat assault.

On 4 May, B Troop, 1/9 Cavalry located the largest weapons cache found during the entire war. B Troop Cobras remained on station the next day when ground elements of the 1st Battalion, 5th Cavalry were inserted to survey and remove the cache. 'The City', as it became known, housed nearly 200 bunkers filled with weapons and supplies.

This B Troop Cobra from the 1/9th Cavalry, coded 'White 23', was photographed at Dau Tieng in 1970. The AH-1G is fitted with at least one XM-159 rocket pod, as well as what appears to be an XM-18 Minigun on the inner stub pylon (*Author's Collection*)

'Pink Teams' of the 1/9 Cav flew cover, maintaining an overhead presence, while troops on the ground removed the supplies.

By this point in the war, each company or troop-sized Cobra unit in the 1st Cavalry Division had been assigned two Cobras fitted with the new XM-35 weapons system, consisting of an M-195 20 mm cannon and two ammunition canisters fitted over the skids. The system was introduced principally to offer a stand-off capability when engaging 0.51-cal anti-aircraft guns. The weapon systems, rushed to Vietnam in late 1969, were now entering widespread frontline service in (*text continues on page 64*)

COLOUR PLATES

1
AH-1G 66-15259
"*Virginia Rose II*" of
Cobra NETT, flown by
Col Paul Anderson
(aircraft commander)
and Maj Nicolas P Stein,
Bien Hoa, September
1967

2
AH-1G 66-15263 of
Cobra NETT, flown by
WO1 John D Thomson
(aircraft commander)
and Gen George Seneff,
Muc Hoa, 8 September
1967

3
AH-1G 66-15272 of the
334th AHC, flown by
Capt Ken Rubin (aircraft
commander) and SP4
Jessie Robertson, Bien
Hoa, 16 November 1967

49

4
AH-1G 67-15464 of B/7/1 Cav, flown by WO1 Len Constantine (aircraft commander) and SP5 Russell Stewart as Crew Chief, Vinh Long, Autumn 1968

5
AH-1G 67-15460 of C/7/1 Cav, flown by CW2 Damon 'Cec' Cecil (aircraft commander), Muc Hoa, Spring 1969

6
AH-1G 67-15651 of C/7/17 Cav, flown by 1Lt Sterling Cox (aircraft commander) and WO1 James Petteys, Plei Djereng, 15 January 1969

7
AH-1G 67-15815
*HAPPINESS IS A WARM
GUN* of the B/9th Avn
Bn, flown by Capt
Robert Schultz (aircraft
commander), Dong Tam,
February 1969

8
AH-1G 67-15??? *VooDo
LADY* of the 11th ACR
(crew unknown), Daub
Ting, April 1969

9
AH-1G 67-15698 of
A/2/17 Cav, flown by
CW2 Len Constantine
(aircraft commander),
A Shau Valley, RVN,
14 May 1969

10
AH-1G 68-15139
SQUATTER SWATTER of
D/1/4 Cav, flown by 1Lt
Dean Sinor (aircraft
commander), Daub Ting,
June 1969

11
AH-1G 68-15146 of the
B/25th Avn Bn, flown by
CW2 Greg Bucy (aircraft
commander) and SP4
Robert Michaels, Cu Chi,
August 1969

12
AH-1G 67-15686 *DDAP*
of D/1/1 Cav, flown by
Capt Mike Henry
(aircraft commander)
and Capt Leo Huber,
Chu Lai, 16 May 1969

52

13
AH-1G 67-15816 'SATAN
10' of the 1st Platoon,
235th AWC, flown by
WO1 Roscoe Armstrong
(aircraft commander),
Can Tho, November
1969

14
AH-1G 67-15762
EXECUTIONER of the
235th AC, flown by Capt
Lou Bouault (aircraft
commander) Daub Ting,
November 1969

15
AH-1G 67-15865 *BLUE
GHOST* of F/8th Cav,
flown by Capt Robert
Wiggins (aircraft
commander), Tam Ky,
January 1970

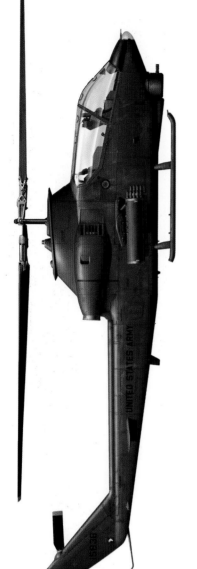

16
AH-1G 67-15838 of A/4/77 ARA, flown by WO1 Robert Sullivan (aircraft commander) and WO1 Tom Damm, Camp Evans, February 1970

17
AH-1G 68-17051 'White 67' of C/2/20 ARA, flown by CW2 Paul Garrity (aircraft commander) and WO1 Jim Nabours, Quan Loi, 24 May 1970

18
AH-1G 68-15049 'White R1' of C/2/20 ARA, flown by 1Lt George Alexander (aircraft commander) and WO1 Jim Moran, Bu Dop, June 1970

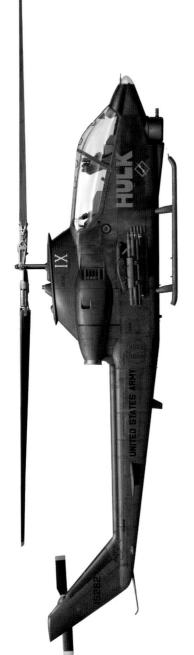

19
AH-1G 66-15262 *HULK* of
D/227 AHB, flown by
WO1 John A Henry
(aircraft commander),
Phuoc Vinh June 1970

20
AH-1G 68-15062 *THE
CRYSTAL SHIP* of C/1/9
Cav, flown by CW2
Walker Jones (aircraft
commander) and SP4
'Mac' McCloy as Crew
Chief, Phuoc Vinh, May
1970

21
AH-1G 68-17068 *CINDY
ANN* of C/1/9 Cav, flown
by CW2 Randy Zahn
(aircraft commander)
and SP4 Marshall
Maring as Crew Chief,
Phuoc Vinh, August
1970

22
AH-1G 69-16437 *Heather Dawn* of C/1/9 Cav, flown by Capt John Craig (aircraft commander), Phuoc Vinh, June 1970

23
AH-1G 69-16439 of A/3/17 Cav, flown by CW2 Dave Tela (aircraft commander), Di An, June 1970

24
AH-1G 68-15209 'White 30' *V.C. BIRTH CONTROL* of the 114th AHC, flown by CW2 Bob Baker (aircraft commander), Vinh Long, 1970

25
AH-1G 68-15074 *Dr Pepper/Kill/RAT PACK* of the 187th AHC, flown by Capt Carl Key (aircraft commander), Tay Ninh, September 1970

26
AH-1G 68-15531 *the Magical Mystery tour* of D/229 AWC, flown by 1Lt Roger Fox (aircraft commander), Quan Loi, 1971

27
AH-1G 68-17054 *Sound of Silence* of C/2/20 ARA, flown by CW2 Jim Moran (aircraft commander) and WO1 Neil MacMillan, LZ Mace, January 1971

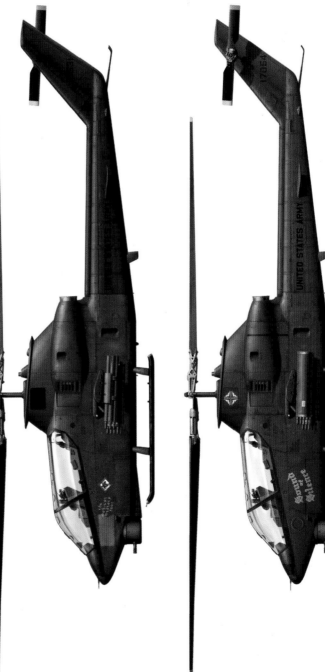

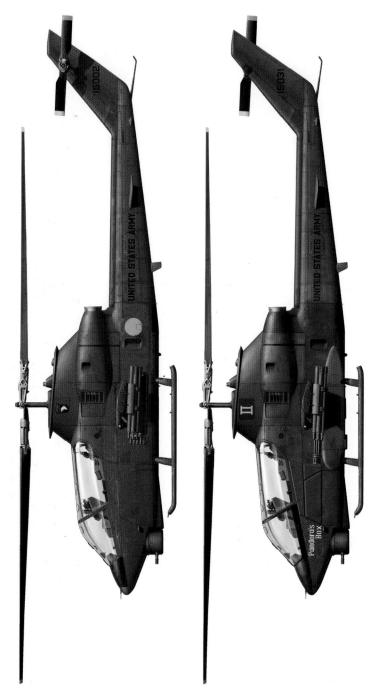

28
AH-1G 68-15002 of D/158 AHB, flown by CW2 Donald Wann (aircraft commander) and 1Lt Paul Magers, Khe Sanh, February

29
AH-1G 68-15031 *Pandora's Box* of the 238th AWC, flown by CW2 Gene Kennedy (aircraft commander), Pleiku, June 1971

30
AH-1G 68-15207 of the 175th AHC, flown by Capt Harris (aircraft commander) and SP4 Jim Stanley, Vinh Long, Summer 1971

31
AH-1G 68-17074 *the
GLADIATOR* of C/16
Cav, flown by WO1 Dan
E Shaver (aircraft
commander), Can Tho,
January 1972

32
AH-1G 68-15012 *#1 DU
ME MI* of F/4 Cav, flown
by CW2 Ken Mick
(aircraft commander),
Hue-Phu Bai, late 1972

33
AH-1G 68-15053 of the
361st AWC, flown by
Capt Bill Reeder (aircraft
commander) and 1Lt
Tim Conry, Camp
Holloway, Pleiku,
9 May 1972

34
AH-1G 67-15725 of F/79
AFA, flown by Capt Mike
Brown (aircraft
commander) and Capt
Marco Cordon, An Loc,
21 June 1972

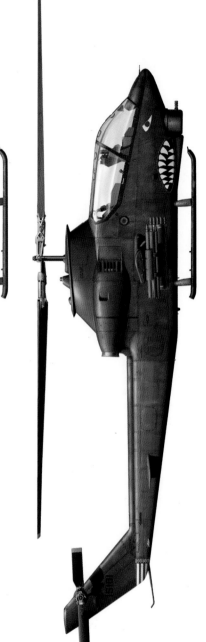

35
AH-1G 68-15101 of H/10
Cav (crew unknown),
Pleiku, Autumn 1972

36
AH-1G 67-15738 of the
129th AHC, flown by
CW2 Ron Paye (aircraft
commander), An Son,
Summer 1972

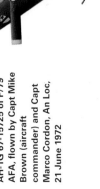

1

2

3

4

5

6

7

8

9

10

12

11

13

14

15

AH-1G 69-16437 *Heather Dawn* undergoes routine maintenance on the breech of its 20 mm cannon in June 1970. Assigned to C/1/9 Cav at Phuoc Vinh, and flown by Capt John Craig, this machine was originally christened *'Betty K'*. However, Capt Craig renamed it when he became aircraft commander in June 1970. *Heather Dawn* saw extensive combat in Cambodia throughout June 1970, and remained with the 1st Cavalry Division until June of the following year, when it was one of the first Cobras assigned to the 173rd AHC at Da Nang. This machine survived the war, and subsequent military service into the late 1980s, until it was retired to the New Jersey Aviation Hall of Fame (*'Mac' McCloy*)

A 2/20th ARA 'Blue Max' Cobra escorts a 'Dustoff' Huey from the 15th Medical Battalion. This shot was taken in May 1970, shortly before the Medal of Honor mission at 'Medevac Meadow' on 24 May (*Jim Moran*)

anticipation of heavy NVA AAA resistance the further US and ARVN troops pushed into Cambodia.

C Troop, 1/9 Cavalry received both of their 20 mm Cobras just before the invasion in late April, AH-1Gs 68-17068 and 69-16437 quickly being adorned with C Troop's stylised sharksmouths. The red platoon leader, Capt Dick Skaaden, was '437's aircraft commander, and he named the Cobra *Betty K*. CW2 Randy Zahn, aircraft commander of 68-17068 *Cindy Ann* from August through March 1971, but still an 'X-ray' during the Cambodian campaign, recalls;

'Most of the learning took place in-theatre. Our job was much different than the likes of the Aerial Rocket Artillery. We had to become expert at map reading, putting in artillery, airstrikes, combat assaults, etc. We flew much more reconnaissance than close air support, as we were the eyes of the division. We were always way out in front of our ground troops, looking for targets for them to exploit. We usually got into a firefight, put in our Blue platoon and if there was anything left of the bad guys, we would put in a full combat assault. When we went into Cambodia we always had a "Rash FAC" (Air Force OV-10 Bronco) with us so we had immediate access to air strikes. When we were over the border, we usually flew a purple team with an UH-1H full of "blues" to secure the aircraft if we went down. For added fire support, we sometimes flew a heavy red team with two AH-1s and a Loach.'

The early gains of the invasion recovered tons of weapons, ammunition and supplies. Within two weeks, however, the NVA rallied and began a series of counterattacks to reclaim or protect cache sites threatened by American units. The 9th ARVN Airborne Brigade engaged elements of the NVA's 7th Division south of Snoul on 23 May and took some light casualties. The 1st Cavalry Division's 15th Medical Battalion was providing 'Dustoff' support for the engaged ARVN units and was called upon to extract wounded paratroopers on the 24th.

'Medevac 2' (UH-1H 67-17485) was despatched with fire-support provided by a team from C Battery, 2/20 ARA. Informed that the LZ was 'cold', Lt Lee Carberreaux made a normal south to north approach for landing. 1Lt George Alexander and WO1 Jim Moran were in AH-1G 68-15049 'Romeo 1' (callsign 'Precise Swords 12'), providing low-altitude close support for the 'Medevac' 'slick' as it flared for landing. As the UH-1 pulled up just above the ground, Alexander broke hard right to cut across the 'slick's' nose to shield it from possible fire from the treeline. Seconds later the Huey and '049 began taking intense heavy automatic weapons fire from multiple directions. 'Medevac 2' then received a fatal hit that completely severed the helicopter's tailboom, leaving Carberreaux powerless to control the stricken UH-1.

UH-1H 'Medevac 8' from the 15th Medical Battalion swoops in to extract 1st Cavalry wounded from a hot LZ 'somewhere in Cambodia' in the summer of 1970. Such missions could not have been contemplated had it not been for the protection offered by AH-1G fire teams

2/20th ARA 'Blue Max' AH-1Gs 68-15049 (with a black tailboom) and 68-15089 sit in the C Troop laager at a muddy Bu Dop, near the Cambodian border. 68-15049 was a participant in the 'Medevac Meadow' mission of 24 May, and is the subject of the cover artwork for this volume (*Jim Moran*)

While 1Lt Alexander broke across 'Medevac 2's' nose, his wingman, CW2 Paul Garrity and front-seater WO1 Jim Nabours (in AH-1G 68-17051), called for the low Cobra to get clear so that he could launch his rockets and commence firing with turret weapons. Alexander circled and climbed for altitude while Moran, in the front seat, continued to lay suppressive

minigun and 40 mm fire on the now-visible bunkers along the treeline.

When the Huey hit the ground, SFC Louis Rocco, a medic serving as an advisor to the 9th ARVN Airborne Brigade, had been thrown clear of the wreckage. Despite a fractured hip and wrist, he climbed back into the burning helicopter to rescue its crew. Finding Sgt Gary Taylor dead, Rocco managed to pull the remaining four crewmen to safety despite his own severe injuries.

Alexander and Garrity remained on station providing suppressive fire on the bunker line until both helicopters had expended their

AH-1G 68-17051 also participated in the 24 May mission, being flown by CW2 Paul Garrity and WO1 Jim Nabours in the high cover role for 'Medevac 2'. This photograph was taken just days after the 'Medevac Meadow' sortie (*Jim Moran*)

One of the myriad missions that 'Blue Max' Cobras were tasked with was bomb damage assessment. Pilot Jim Moran snapped this photograph from his AH-1G as he overflew the remnants of a heavily bombed 'Medevac Meadow' on 26 May 1970 (*Jim Moran*)

The 187th AHC's Capt Carl Key and WO1 Steve Wescoat pose with their AH-1G (68-15074 *Dr Pepper/Kill/RAT PACK*) at Tay Ninh in late 1970. This particular helicopter was the first right-hand tail-rotored Cobra assigned to the 187th (*D Parchuk collection*)

ammunition. Heavy fighting continued in the LZ, and additional 'Blue Max' Cobras were called in to support the downed 'Medevac' and elements of the 9th ARVN Airborne Brigade trapped nearby. A fire team led by CW2 Mac Cookson relieved the battered Cobras on station, and continued support until sundown.

Attempts to extract the downed crew and wounded ARVN paratroopers met with fierce resistance, severely damaging three additional Hueys, before rescue efforts were suspended for the night. SFC Rocco organised the group's defence and kept his crew alive and alert until morning, when elements of the 229th Assault Helicopter Battalion, supported by all 12 Cobras of C Battery, were able to pull them out. For his actions on 24-25 May 1970 at 'Medevac Meadow', SFC Louis Rocco was awarded the Medal of Honor.

Ultimately, the Cambodian incursion was limited by political factors, and American units were not permitted to press more than 20 miles into the newly-invaded country, which allowed some NVA/VC units to escape to safety during the operation. Brilliant use of airmobile assets in the opening stages allowed the invasion force to seize key points well inside Cambodia, and the effective employment of the invasion force's Cobras enabled airborne troops to land nearly unopposed in all cases. The initial gains allowed Allied units to capture massive amounts of supplies, thus dealing a serious blow to NVA/VC operations in South Vietnam.

The 235th AC had a significantly different experience in Cambodia. The new company commander, Capt Lou Bouault (formerly company commander of B/1st Aviation Battalion, dubbed the 'Rebels'), had rebuilt the 235th in the spring of 1970, changing the unit's tactics and boosting morale. It had previously been held back by a minimum altitude restriction, which negated the Cobra's ability to accurately place rocket fire in support of friendly troops. After Bouault took command in March, he emphasised low-level attack flying just a few feet off the ground. According to Bouault, Cambodia was 'almost enjoyable, since the enemy usually knew we were coming and would disappear, leaving large quantities of supplies, fuel and ammunition for us to destroy virtually at will.'

By the end of June, due to increasing pressure in the US, all American units were ordered out of Cambodia. The incursion netted nearly two million rounds of 7.62 mm ammunition, thousands of grenades, rockets and explosives and thousands of tons of rice. The 87 Cobras of the 1st Cavalry Division that were committed to the incursion fired 92,016 2.75-in rockets and nearly a million of the 6,167,645 7.62 mm rounds fired by the division during its the two months in Cambodia. The division killed over 2500 NVA soldiers, a large percentage of these falling to the awesome firepower of the AH-1.

INCREMENT V WITHDRAWAL – TWO DIVISIONS

The remainder of 1970 seemed almost anti-climactic after the successes of the Cambodian operation. American involvement continued to wind down despite the US government's concerns over the ARVN's ability to defend South Vietnam.

Two Cobra units within the 1st Cavalry Division were reorganised in November, eliminating D Company 227th AHB and reorganising it as E Troop, 9th Cavalry. D/229th still retained its Assault Helicopter designation, but it was also reorganised as an Air Cav troop to augment the already over extended cavalry squadron.

December would bring yet another blow to US troop strength in South Vietnam when both the 4th and 25th Divisions were sent back to the US, further decreasing the number of combat-capable Cobras in Vietnam by a significant number. The 'Gambler Guns' and 'Diamond Heads' both returned stateside with their respective divisions, while the division reconnaissance units – D/1/10 and D/3/4 – both remained in Vietnam as independent cavalry troops for II and III Corps.

The year had brought a great deal of success with the Cambodian invasion, but also frustration with a sense that this mission had not been accomplished. The largest heliborne assault of the war, spearheaded by Cobra fire teams, had netted tons of supplies, weapons and enemy casualties, yet the war showed no sign of coming to a close.

AH-1G 67-15594 provides the backdrop for an unnamed soldier at a forward base in early 1970. As with all D/227 Cobras, the last three digits of this aircraft's serial number have been stencilled in yellow immediately in front of the windscreen (*Author's collection*)

ARVN troops and a trio of 'Delta Devils' gather in front of a 235th AWC Cobra prior to launching an aerial assault into Cambodia in the late summer of 1970 (*Roscoe Armstrong*)

Amongst the first Cobras to arrive in Vietnam, AH-1G 66-15262 *HULK* of D/227 AHB had been refitted with an M-28 turret in place of the original Emerson TAT-102A system by the time of its participation in the invasion of Cambodia in late April 1970. Photographed in June 1970 at Phuoc Vinh with its assigned pilot, WO1 John A Henry, at the controls, *HULK* was one of several colourfully marked 'El Lobo' AH-1s to see action in the Cambodian campaign (*John Conway*)

1971 – VIETNAMIZATION

With the withdrawal of US infantry divisions from Vietnam in 1969-70, American combat strength had dwindled significantly. The two US airmobile divisions (1st Cavalry and 101st Airborne), a single infantry division (the AMERICAL division) and an independent cavalry regiment remained in-country, although they were all slated to return to the United States during the next phase of withdrawals in 1971.

In III Corps, major offensive operations had all but ceased. 1st Cavalry Division Long Range Reconnaissance Patrol (LRRP) operations continued, both in support of the division and the ARVN units in the AO. These missions were usually assigned a 'Blue Max' Cobra fire team as gun cover during insertions and extractions.

On 21 January an LRRP team from H Company, 75th Rangers had set up a night defensive position on a well-camouflaged NVA bunker complex in western III Corps. During the night, a large NVA unit moved back into the area and the LRRP team leader decided to get out. The soldiers were discovered while radioing for an extraction and were soon fighting for their lives. Night and bad weather made the situation worse. The 'hot' section of 'Blue Max' AH-1s, led by Scott Fenwick, was scrambled from LZ Mace and was on station within minutes, firing at NVA forces in the area. AH-1 pilot Jim Moran remembers;

'Fenwick came on station and started shooting in support of the LRRP withdrawal, but there were so many bad guys running around, the LRRP couldn't get out. Fenwick radioed back to Bear Cat that he was expended and low on fuel. He recommended another section be scrambled to continue to provide gun cover to the LRRP. I was sitting in the club minding my own business when the Battery

CW2 Jim Moran prepares to lift off from LZ Mace in AH-1G *Sound of Silence* (68-17054) in early 1971. He and WO1 Neil MacMillan used this Cobra on the LRRP extraction mission on 21 January 1971 that saw Moran recommended for a Silver Star. Although slated to DEROS (Date of Expected Return from OverSeas) within the next few days, Moran accepted the mission and maintained control of an increasingly dangerous situation at night, and in bad weather, until the LRRP team had been safely extracted. One of the longest AH-1G missions of war, Moran remembers making 'the perimeter at LZ Mace on fumes in the gas tank' (*Jim Moran*)

Bone dome on and microphone plugged in, CW2 Jim Moran is seen in his 'office'– the aircraft commander's seat of *Sound of Silence* – in 1971 (*Jim Moran*)

Sound of Silence's crew chief enjoys a cigarette whilst perched on the cockpit sill. His right arm is resting on the pilot's cockpit armour (*Jim Moran*)

CO, Capt Bob Lund, approached me and said he needed me to go to Mace to relieve Fenwick's section. I pointed out that there was a rather nasty frontal system between Bear Cat and Mace, and that I didn't have an aircraft assigned that night. He said I could have any bird I wanted, a front-seater (I volunteered Neil MacMillan) and a wingman, and to get moving. He also told me that since I was our "most experienced aircraft commander and nightfighter", I should be resourceful enough to solve the weather problem and get to Mace!

'After taking off (in 68-17054), it became apparent that we were not going to get through the weather at any altitude the Cobra was capable of attaining. Even if we did, there was Nui Chua Chan – 876 metres of solid granite – waiting out there in the dark. I did the only thing I could think of and led us down Highway QL1 at below tree top level. We could see the road, and because we flew the route every time we went to Mace, I knew there were no wires. All we had to do was hope that no one was coming in the opposite direction. We broke out of the weather at the point where QL1 takes a right and heads for the coast.

'We had no trouble locating the LRRP team because Fenwick was filling the sky with flares from a nearby 105 mm battery and a VNAF C-47 that was orbiting overhead. There were green tracers zipping up in sporadic bursts at the lights from Fenwick's section. It was a show-and-a-half!

'I was talking to Fenwick on the UHF, and it quickly became apparent that things were as bad as they looked. He had tried to get a lift in to snatch the LRRP, but because of the bad weather he got no takers. I took over the mission, contacted the LRRP for a situation report and took a mental inventory of everything that was in the air. I decided we needed to do something fast, so I got the gun artillery to move the flares away from our airspace for safety reasons. Through some miracle we got the C-47 crew to stop dropping their flares as well, and I then set about calming down the LRRP. I had my wingman turn out his lights and go down low to make noise and scare the NVA. That pissed them off, and they tossed some wild anti-aircraft fire at him. Their fire was way behind him so he didn't see it. If he had, he would have crapped his pants – there was a lot of it!

'A Huey then came on station at 4000 ft and wanted to know if he could help. I let him know that I needed an emergency extraction and asked if he had ropes or a McGuire rig. Turned out he was a C&C bird, with some unit commander and his staff on board. He couldn't haul anyone out of a clear LZ, let alone make a hovering extraction under fire! While all this was going on, we continued to lay rockets down on the area to worry the bad guys, and to keep the faith with our guys on the ground.

'I asked the C&C bird to see if he could radio somebody for an emergency extraction. He had no luck. I then remembered that the 15th Med kept a bird from Charlie Company at LZ Mace. I got on the horn and with a stroke of luck got hold of my old buddy Capt Monty Halcomb ("Medevac 8"). He had a hoist with a jungle penetrator on it, which would be ideal for the mission. Monty informed me that what I wanted to do was illegal, against regulations and would get us all in trouble. It seems there was a rule against using Air Ambulance assets to transport uninjured personnel. I told him those guys were *going* to be injured or worse if he didn't come, and that I had tried to get a "slick" without success; Monty agreed.

'While all this was going on, we were still directing artillery, and talking to the guys on the ground. I told them of my plan, and that we needed them to move in to a thinner cluster of trees that my wingman had spotted. By this time their flashlights were kaput, so I told them to burn a bit of C-4 gas in a steel pot to mark their location while we shot up the area around them. The LRRP guy on the radio thought that I was crazy, and said as much, since the glow would give their position away. I simply suggested to him that "Mr NVA" already knew that he was there. He must have been shocked by my reply because he very quietly said "Okay". I don't know where the idea came from, but I asked if he had blown his claymore mines yet. He said he forgot to in all the confusion.

'Medevac duly arrived, and I told the LRRP to dump everything except its weapons and radio and set up for the show. Just at that instant, the artillery guy radioed that he was shutting down the flares and harassing fire to conserve ammo for his night H&I (Harassing & Interdiction – an artillery mission which fired a few rounds into suspected areas of enemy activity) mission. I blew out a stream of expletives in his direction and said I'd show him some H&Is he'd never forget if I didn't keep getting his support. He stayed with us.

'We got the LRRP to blow the mines and scoot 30 or 40 metres to a spot where Monty Halcomb was able to swoop in and start hauling them up. The NVA must have crapped when those claymores went off because our guys ran right by some and never drew a look! Monty got a few out on the hoist, but he was overloaded and was straining his machine to keep it in the air. My wingman (Joe Perez) saw a clearing big enough to put a chopper in that was away from the action. We decided to drop off the guys on the Medevac with one of the M-60s and go back and get the rest of them. Monty headed for the new LZ, but before he could get back, a 227th 'slick' had decided to investigate the fireworks. He came up on "Guard" and we moved him to our VHF frequency. I could have kissed the son-of-a-bitch, as he had a rope ladder! I sent Monty to get the guys he had dropped in the clearing and the 227th driver went in and pulled the RTO and LRRP team leader out of the fire.

'I remember laughing when the RTO (dangling at the end of 50-ft rope ladder) called and asked if we could slow the ride down a bit. We dumped the rest of our ammo on the area, told the artillery boys goodnight and turned for home. We made the perimeter at Mace on fumes in the gas tank. My flight suit was drenched from the hips up. It turned out that the LRRP commander – a major – had listened to the entire operation on his radio and recommended us for the Silver Star.'

OPERATION *DEWEY CANYON II/LAM SON 719*

The Vietnamization of the war was well underway by January 1971. American combat units were winding up offensive operations and were fast becoming relegated to second-line status, or at least that was the

An A Battery, 4/77th ARA AH-1 takes off in support of Operation *Lam Son 719* (the Allied invasion of Laos) in late January 1971 (*Barry Martens*)

A Battery, 4/77th 'Dragons' pilot WO1 Barry Martens is seen with his AH-1 at Khe Sanh in the midst of *Lam Son 719* (*Barry Martens*)

intention. While some South Vietnamese units were doing a much greater job of taking the war to the enemy, American combat units were still seeing a great deal of fighting, particularly Air Cavalry squadrons.

January saw much high level planning taking place for a major South Vietnamese offensive into Laos to seize several key supply points along the Ho Chi Minh trail. The operation was to have four distinct phases, the first of which, Operation *Dewey Canyon II* (known as *Lam Son 719* to the ARVN) would be conducted by US ground and aviation assets in an effort to open Highway QL9 so as to enable ARVN ground units to attack across the border.

Dewey Canyon II, scheduled to commence on 29 January, would be spearheaded by the 1st Brigade, 5th Mechanized Infantry Division, under the control of the 101st Airborne Division. D Troop, 3/5 Cavalry provided the reconnaissance elements, using 'hunter-killer' AH-1/OH-6 teams to lead the brigade along the mountainous route QL9 to the old Marine base at Khe Sanh and then on to the Laotian border. The advance took three days, and although casualties were fairly light, terrain and weather took their toll on the advancing task force.

At 1130 hrs on the 31st, QL9 was declared open, beginning a massive westward flow of men and materiel in I Corps. Phase I continued until 9 February, and consisted of small unit actions along the border. The Air Cav's mission was to locate possible LZs and support Command and Control North Reconnaissance teams – MACV-SOG was split into three Command and Control sectors, CCN, CCC and CCS. For the remainder of the campaign, the 1st Brigade, 5th Division held the border area along QL9, but did not venture into Laos.

As Phase II began, air assets for *Lam Son 719* came north to I Corps from all four Corps areas. As with the Cambodian invasion of the previous year, an airmobile division, in this case the 101st Airborne, formed the core of the helicopter task force. The eight air cavalry troops participating in the operation were placed under the operational control of 2/17th Cavalry, led by Lt Robert Molinelli. As with previous operations, the Air Cav would be the lead elements of the operation.

The first loss of the campaign was AH-1G 66-15340 from D/3/5 on 5 February. WO1 Carl Wood and his front-seater, WO1 James Paul, were flying as gun cover for the extraction of a CCN Reconnaissance team west of Khe Sanh. Poor weather had been a factor in the early stages of the operation, and continued to be so throughout February. During the extraction, Wood's Cobra entered heavy IFR conditions, and whilst attempting to climb out of the clouds the AH-1 crashed into a nearby mountainside, killing both crewmen. The remaining aircraft on the mission immediately began searching for survivors and quickly found the crash site.

Phase II began on 10 February when the ARVN's 1st Corps launched its heliborne assault across the border – several Cobra units from outside I Corps were moved to the region to provide additional firepower for the assault

force. The 235th AWC and B/7/1 were OPCONed (Operationally Controlled – one unit being placed under the control of another) to the 101st Airborne Division from IV Corps, while the 1st Cavalry Division sent B/2/20 ARA and D/227 (E/1/9 Cav) to reinforce the 4/77 and D/158 respectively. Each US aviation unit was assigned a specific ARVN counterpart to support throughout the campaign.

The 1st ARVN Infantry Division was air assaulted into LZs Hotel and Blue, south of QL9, with gun cover from the 'Redskins' of D/158th AHB. 'Pink Teams' from B/7/1 and A/2/17 Cavalry led the way for the ARVN Airborne and Ranger units being inserted at LZ Ranger South, while C/2/17 and C/7/17 covered Ranger North. Soon after the initial assaults, it was determined that the OH-6 did not have the range or survivability to operate in the mountains of Laos. A new reconnaissance team was therefore hastily created, with Cobras operating as armed scouts in heavy fire teams of three aircraft alongside a C&C UH-1.

The North Vietnamese knew the ARVN units were coming, and had placed 14 AAA battalions in and around the intended LZs. Helicopter losses were heavy, and would continue to be throughout

Wearing an all too typical look synonymous with pilots standing a seemingly endless alert, WO1 Tony Hoffman of A Battery, 4/77th awaits the call to action at Khe Sanh (*Barry Martens*)

This 'Dragons' AH-1G (67-15649) received the 20 mm gun upgrade, but it is seen here without the fuselage ammunition containers or the cannon. Instead, it is carrying two XM-159 19-shot rocket pods. The helicopter was also retro-fitted with an Environmental Control Unit (air conditioning) in the field (*Barry Martens*)

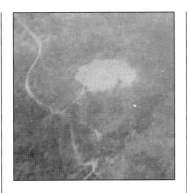

This rare shot provides an overhead view of LZ 31, where 101st Airborne and C/7/17 Cobras engaged NVA armour that was overrunning the landing zone on 25 February 1971 (*Barry Martens*)

the operation. Anti-aircraft fire from both 37 mm and 57 mm weapons was frequent, and it steadily took its toll. On the opening day, 12 helicopters were damaged or destroyed, and 48 hours later two Cobras from C/2/17 were shot down.

The 159th ASHB was tasked with recovering downed helicopters and returning them to South Vietnam to be repaired and rebuilt. And thanks to the heavy AAA encountered during this operation, the 'Playtex' CH-47s were extremely busy making numerous trips across the border into Laos. Old UH-1Cs were written off as obsolete and not worth recovering, but the Cobra was a valuable piece of hardware, and every effort was made to return the damaged airframes to South Vietnam for repair. However, they were complicated to sling and needed a drogue chute to stabilise them in flight, otherwise they would start to spin under the Chinook.

A 'Hook' pilot involved in the Laos campaign of 1971 stated, 'I can honestly say that I don't remember a time when a Chinook returned from Khe Sanh for the evening without a Huey or a Cobra slung under it for the repair yards. Sometimes I'd make two trips late in the afternoon. Those ships were really shot to pieces!'

ARVN units made significant progress on the ground, capturing large weapons caches and engaging in heavy combat. Their losses were significant, however. To downed American aviators, the 'Hoc Bao' or 'Black Cat' assault groups were a godsend.

Due to the Cooper-Church Amendment, American combat troops were not allowed into Laos. Therefore, the Aero-rifle platoons of the Air Cav squadrons, which normally served as a quick reaction force trained to rescue downed crews, were left out of the action. The 'Hoc Bao' took up this

A C Troop, 7/17 Cavalry Cobra heads west towards the Laotian border in 1971 (*Steve Shepard*)

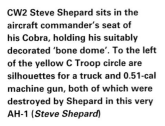

CW2 Steve Shepard sits in the aircraft commander's seat of his Cobra, holding his suitably decorated 'bone dome'. To the left of the yellow C Troop circle are silhouettes for a truck and 0.51-cal machine gun, both of which were destroyed by Shepard in this very AH-1 (*Steve Shepard*)

mission with enthusiasm, successfully extracting several downed
aircrews during the campaign.

Such a rescue took place on
25 February, after a heavy fire
team from C/7/17 was despatched
from Khe Sanh to defend LZ 31,
which was being overrun by NVA
armour. When the 'Yellow Scarf'
fire team arrived on scene, USAF
Phantom IIs were in the process of
completing their bombing runs.

F-4D s/n 66-8691, crewed by Maj Richard Smith and Capt J S Talley,
was hit by AAA fire on its fourth pass and the crew ejected. Pilot Smith
was killed, probably by the initial AAA hits, but the fire team's C&C
ship quickly swooped in and rescued Capt Talley.

This D/101st Aviation Battalion AH-1, armed with a 20 mm cannon, three seven-shot rocket pods and the nose turret, attempted to take off from Khe Sanh overloaded with ammunition and fuel. Due to the density altitude and the aircraft's gross weight, the helicopter's engine did not have enough power to lift the AH-1 and it settled hard, with the main rotor striking the runway (*Barry Martens*)

The main objective of the entire Laos operation was the capture of
the city of Tchepone, which was accomplished on 6 March. The final
withdrawal phase of *Lam Son 719* began shortly thereafter, again
supported by US aircraft. The NVA followed, making movement back
to South Vietnam very difficult. As the last of the ARVN's 4th
Battalion 1st Infantry were pulling back eastwards, remnants of the
force became trapped by the NVA in a bomb crater. Capt Keith
Brandt (callsign 'Music 16') from D/101 answered a call for close air
support, and leading a fire team, he moved in to assess the situation.
The ARVN soldiers radioed that they were surrounded, and marked
their position with smoke.

4/1 Battalion had entered Laos with 420 men, and after six weeks of
heavy fighting just 88 remained, 61 of whom were wounded. An
English-speaking sergeant, callsign 'Whiskey', was in command, and
he assisted in directing Brandt's fire. 'Music 16' remained on station
over the trapped ARVN unit all afternoon, leaving three times to refuel
and rearm. Acting as armed scouts, Brandt's fire team came in low and
fast in order to pinpoint NVA troop concentrations, thus maximising
the effect of the AH-1's firepower.

By 1700 hrs, lift ships from the 173rd had commenced their
extraction of the beleaguered 4/1 ARVN. As he led the lift ships in to
the LZ, Brandt took heavy fire and aborted his approach. At this point
he lost his hydraulics, but the AH-1 pilot nevertheless attempted to
make another strafing run in an effort to guide the lift ships in. When
he realised this was impossible, Brandt directed them verbally, and then
tried to get to the relative safety of the Xe Pon River. As he turned, fire
engulfed the rotor mast and spread rapidly, his Cobra crashing in a ball
of flame. His last transmission was, 'Give my love to my wife and family'. Capt Keith Brandt and his front-seater, 1Lt Albert Boffman, were
listed as MIA until 1990, when their remains were returned to the US.

Of the 88 ARVN soldiers in the crater, only 36 made it back to
Vietnam alive. The 173rd's 'slicks' were overloaded and strained to
stay aloft. As the UH-1s extracted, those that were in danger of being
left behind hung on to the Hueys' skids in a final desperate attempt to
get out.

Lam Son 719 was declared a victory because a large quantity of NVA supplies was captured and destroyed and staggering casualties were inflicted on the enemy. US forces lost more than 100 helicopters during the operation, with 600+ damaged. Considering the number of sorties flown during the six-week long Laos campaign, losses were staggeringly low. Gunship sorties, in support of both US and ARVN troops in Phases I, II and III, totalled 34,173. Cobra losses were 26 aircraft destroyed and 158 damaged.

PHASE VI WITHDRAWAL

After seven years of combat and operations in all four Corps Tactical Zones, the 1st Cavalry Division ceased operations in Vietnam during the final week of April 1971 as part of the Phase VI redeployment. The division's 3rd Brigade would stay in Vietnam for another 14 months, continuing to fly both offensive and defensive heliborne operations.

D/227th had a brief stay with the 3rd Brigade as the newly converted E Troop 1/9 Cavalry in May 1971. The 'El Lobos' retained their old unit callsign, but would function as a part of the 'mini-cav division' that the 3rd Brigade had been transformed into. The Troop was only attached to 3rd Brigade for a month, before being deactivated and sent back to the US. Two batteries of the 'Blue Max' ARA would also head home within the next four months, leaving C Battery with 3rd Brigade, who in turn redesignated it F Battery, 79th Aerial Field Artillery in August. As with E Troop, the 'Blue Max' callsign would again be retained by F Battery. Operations in these closing days were limited to support of ARVN forces, and local 'hunter-killer' missions around III Corps.

NEW CONVERSIONS

After *Lam Son 719*, B Battery 2/20 ARA did not return to III Corps. Personnel and aircraft were reassigned as needed throughout Vietnam, and as units left for home, their AH-1s were often turned over to other units remaining in-country. Of the 12 aircraft that B Battery came to I Corps with, seven were turned over to I Corps-based units to replace losses. The remaining five aircraft returned to III Corps to replace attrition in A and C Batteries.

The 238th AC had acquired its first two Cobras in January 1971 (most likely 66-15258 and 67-15801), but because of planning for *Lam Son 719*, II Corps decided to hold off on conversion until after the operation. The unit received the remainder of its assigned Cobras in June, immediately initiating operations throughout II Corps. Missions usually consisted of convoy escort and standing alert to support ARVN infantry in the area. The 238th AWC's CW2 Gene Kennedy flew a great number of these sorties, and remembers;

'After a long day on standby boring holes in the sky over convoys, no Cobra team wanted to come home with a full load of ammo, least of all me. So we would call "Mike FAC" and see what he had going. On one particular day, I was flying lead, with Leon LaPorte on my wing. "Mike FAC" had something going west of our base, so we went out to help. As we approached, a team of A-1Es was finishing up, and then we watched a team of A-7s hit the same target – a cave in the side

of the mountain that the FAC had found. Next in line was a team of F-4s, but they weren't on location yet, so "Mike FAC" let us have a shot at it. On the second pass, Leon put a 2.75-in rocket down the mouth of the cave and got the most hellacious secondary explosions you ever saw! Send the F-4s home with a full load – the Cobras took care of it!'

Withdrawal of US combat units continued throughout the year. IV Corps lost the 235th AC to force reductions, and with that, a significant amount of firepower in the Delta region. The 1st Brigade, 5th Mechanized Division was sent home in August, along with the final elements of 1st and 2nd Brigades from the 1st Cav Division. C Battery, 2/20 ARA was then reorganised with Cobras from all three batteries and redesignated F Battery, 79th Aerial Field Artillery (AFA). 'Blue Max' would soldier on, providing fire support to ARVN and US units until late 1972, when they were withdrawn.

The final withdrawal of US combat units in 1971 occurred in November, when the AMERICAL Division pulled out. The divisional reconnaissance squadrons – F/8th Cav and D/1/1 Cav – remained in I Corps, coming under the direct control of II Field Force. Three of the 'Warlords' Cobras from 123rd Aviation were reassigned to the 'Blue Ghosts' and 'Swords' as replacement aircraft. The remainder returned to the US with the division.

Combat operations in Vietnam seemed to be winding down as 1971 drew to a close. The remaining US combat units were getting ready for withdrawal and no longer focusing on combat operations. Supplies and materiel began to flow towards the coast, instead of away from the major ports. There was a sense that the war was ending and the NVA was beaten. The following year would provide the South Vietnamese and US governments with a rude awakening.

The 238th AWC acquired 12 Cobras in June 1971 and quickly initiated operations (typically convoy escort and standing alert in support of ARVN infantry in the area) in II Corps. This aircraft (68-15031 *Pandora's Box*), seen in its new 238th AWC 'Gunrunners' colours in the summer of 1971, had initially served with B/2/20 ARA until the Cav left Vietnam in April 1971. 68-15031 was transferred once again in December of that same year, when it became part of the newly formed 60th AHC (*Gene Kennedy*)

1972 – INVASION FROM THE NORTH

January 1972 was eventful for the remaining Cobra units in Vietnam. The 101st Airborne Division had been notified of its impending withdrawal and had begun sending units back to the US the previous month, beginning with the 3/5th Cav and 158th Aviation Battalion. The 4/77th ARA would follow by battery during December and January. A Battery was the last to depart, turning half of its machines over to the F/79th AFA 'Blue Max'. The 238th AWC also stood down in January, passing its AH-1s on to the new 60th AHC 'Ghostriders'.

By March, the entire 101st Airborne Division had stood down and returned to America as part of increment X of the US withdrawal. The 101st was the final US division to leave Vietnam, leaving all remaining Cobra units in-country under the control of the 1st Aviation Brigade.

EASTER OFFENSIVE

The NVA crossed the Demilitarized Zone (DMZ) under favourable weather conditions in the early hours of 30 March 1972. Monsoon weather severely hampered flight operations, allowing the NVA to move tanks, APCs and the equivalent of three infantry divisions with full artillery and air defences across the border with near impunity in the initial stages of the operation.

Once the weather improved, 'Blue Ghost' Cobras were heavily engaged throughout the First Regional Assistance Command (FRAC), formerly known as I Corps. On 2 April, a USAF EB-66 Destroyer (callsign 'BAT 21') electronic warfare aircraft was downed by a North Vietnamese SA-2 missile over the DMZ. Its navigator, Lt Col Iceal Hambleton (callsign 'BAT 21 Bravo'), managed to eject from the disintegrating aircraft and landed outside Cam Lo – a town just south of the DMZ that had already been overrun by NVA units.

A USAF 0-2A FAC (callsign 'Bilk 34') had been on station when the jet was lost, and its pilot had monitored the ejection. He then called for all available assets to head for the area in an effort to recover the downed crewman. 'Blue Ghost 39', alias UH-1H 67-17801 piloted by WO1 John W Frink, along with AH-1s 'Blue Ghost 24' and '28' (flown by WO1 George Ezell and Capt Mike Rosebeary, respectively) were despatched from Hue-Phu Bai to attempt a rescue of 'BAT 21 Bravo'. After being informed that up to six crewmembers from the EB-66 could be on the ground, Capt Rosebeary called for his reserve UH-1, 'Blue Ghost 30', to join the mission. Rosebeary was instructed not to fly north of the Dong Ha River due to large enemy formations and heavy AAA.

Taking a risk, Capt Rosebeary instructed 'Blue Ghost 24' to turn back and escort 'Blue Ghost 30', which was trying to catch up with the formation. Splitting the flight greatly reduced the AH-1s' ability to provide covering fire for the Huey extractions, and also served to leave the Cobra crews vulnerable to AAA after making their firing passes.

Rosebeary followed 'Blue Ghost 39' in to the extraction point at low altitude in a high trail formation so as to provide covering fire for the 'slick'. However, things began to go sour as they passed over the northern bank of the Dong Ha River, the AH-1 being subjected to unrelenting ground fire. Rosebeary hit back with rockets and 40 mm grenades, but ground fire was coming up from all around him and both helicopters quickly began to take a lot of hits.

With his warning panel lit up like a Christmas tree, Rosebeary called for 'Blue Ghost 39' to return to base while he attempted to nurse his stricken Cobra back home as well. As he banked around, 'Blue Ghost 39' began to turn as well, but lost altitude and hit the ground hard, taking fire all the way down. Realising the 'slick' had crashed in enemy territory, Rosebeary radioed the other team, which was rapidly heading north, not to cross the river. He then contacted a USAF HH-53 and reported that he was heading south, but would be going down when the engine quit. He and his front-seater, WO1 Charles Gorski, were immediately picked up by the waiting HH-53, 'Jolly Green 67'.

By this time it was dark, further complicating the chances of an immediate rescue of both 'Blue Ghost 39' and 'BAT 21 Bravo'. Capt Sprouse, accompanied by Lt LaCelle, escorted 'Blue Ghost 30' north to attempt a rescue, regardless of the time or the bad weather closing in. The three helicopters were unable to make contact with the downed crews due to heavy cloud cover, and they spent the night at FSB Bastogne – an old 101st Airborne firebase held by the ARVN.

'BAT 21 Bravo' Lt Col Hambleton would eventually be rescued 11 days later by Lt Thomas Norris and Nguyen Van Kiet (US and Vietnamese Navy SEALs) and extracted aboard a sampan down the Song Mieu Giang River. Some 234 medals were awarded to individuals from the Army, Air Force and Navy for this rescue, and Lt Norris received the Medal of Honor for his role in the operation.

THINGS TO COME – BGM-71 TOW

In the first week of May 1972, a new weapons system was tested with impressive results. Ironically, the state-of-the-art BGM-71 TOW (Tube-launched Optically-tracked Wire-guided missile) system was not carried by the AH-1G, but on a number of near-obsolete UH-1B gunships flown by the 1st and 2nd TOW detachments out of Pleiku.

NVA forces attacked into II Corps, now known as SRAC (Corps areas were renamed in 1972, with I to III Corps becoming the First to Third Regional Assistance Commands, while IV Corps became the Delta Regional Assistance Command), with a combined arms team of tanks and infantry. The 'Hawks Claw' UH-1/TOW combination was first fired against this threat on 2 May when missiles destroyed four captured US-made M-41 tanks and a 105 mm artillery piece. The 361st AWC once again flawlessly performed its role of armed escort, covering the 'Hawk's Claw' UH-1s during the few vulnerable seconds

A 'Hawk's Claw' UH-1B Huey of the 1st TOW Test Detachment sits on the ramp at Camp Holloway (Pleiku) in May 1972. The BGM-71 TOW (Tube-launched Optically-tracked Wire-guided missile) system Hueys were escorted by Cobras of the 361st AWC on all of their missions – an interesting portent of the future of the Cobra's combat career with the deadly TOW system (*VHPA*)

after launch when they had to stay locked onto the target. 'Pink Panthers' Cobras escorted the UH-1B/TOW birds on every combat sortie in the SRAC, and provided suppressive fire against anti-aircraft weapons while the TOW birds eliminated the armoured threat to ARVN troops on the ground.

The performance of the TOW system in Vietnam against armoured threats during May and June 1972 effectively sealed the fate of the AH-56 Cheyenne programme, the proposed TOW Cobra negating the need for the far more complex, and expensive, Cheyenne.

Aside from TOW escort missions, the 361st AWC also flew conventional ground support missions throughout April and May. On 9 May, Capt Bill Reeder (a 'Panthers' platoon leader) was leading a fire team in support of ARVN units west of Kontum. The special forces camp at Ben Het was under attack by NVA tanks, and Reeder's team was escorting a 57th AHC Huey loaded with LAW rockets that was heading for the camp on a resupply mission. Upon entering the area, Reeder's Cobra began taking hits, while the 'Slick' got in and was able to unload. Reeder's engine was struck several times, crippling the Cobra and forcing him to set down hard. The AH-1 began to burn upon hitting the ground.

As he began his descent, Reeder's wingman, WO1 Steve 'Flame' Allen, fired a pair of flechette rockets into Reeder's intended LZ to eliminate any enemy infantry in the area. Just after firing his rockets, Allen came under intense 0.51-cal fire and was hit in the chest. His front-seater, Capt Bob Gamber, immediately took control of the stricken Cobra and managed to fly it to safety. Allen was transferred to the C&C ship and medevaced to the hospital at Pleiku, while Gamber returned to the fight in the back seat of his Cobra.

Meanwhile, Capt Reeder, and his front-seater 1Lt Tim Conry, had managed to get out of the crashed Cobra just as it began to burn. Conry crawled a few feet away from the wreckage before passing out from his injuries. As Capt Reeder was attempting to get out of the flaming wreckage, his survival vest hung up on the seat armour, suspending him inverted outside the aircraft. Struggling to get free, Reeder was finally thrown clear of the wrecked AH-1 when the flames reached the fuel tank and it exploded.

A second Cobra team had by then been despatched to Ben Het, this time escorting a 'Hawk's Claw' TOW Huey that had been tasked with knocking out enemy armour. By the time they reached Reeder's crash site, the AH-1 was little more than a pile of white ash with a tail boom.

US advisors at Ben Het had reported seeing the front-seater get out of the Cobra alive. Concerned that the pilot, who appeared to be hung up in the cockpit, may burn to death, one of the advisors had raised his rifle to end Reeder's suffering, but the Cobra exploded before he could fire a shot. When the smoke cleared, there was no sign of the pilot.

An air cav rescue team from H/17th Cav was standing by, but was not permitted into the area to search for survivors until nightfall. Reeder had made it to the treeline and watched as an OH-6 came in and found Lt Conry. According to the Loach pilot, Conry was alive when he was picked up, but had died by the time they reached the hospital. Reeder was not able to make the Loach aware of his presence due to the extent of his injuries – the pilot had a broken back and ankle. He was able to evade capture for three days, however, but was eventually captured by five NVA soldiers.

Capt Reeder's 11 months in captivity began with three days of interrogations followed by a forced march into northern Cambodia. During his interrogation, Reeder was told to sign confessions that he'd dropped chemical and biological weapons on Vietnam, which he refused to do. The pilot was eventually marched north into Vietnam, and he spent the remainder of his captivity at Hoa Lo Prison – the infamous 'Hanoi Hilton'. Reeder returned to the US in March 1973.

AN LOC – CAVALRY TO THE RESCUE

As units in the First and Second Regional Assistance Command were engaging infantry and armoured units pouring over the border, the NVA's 9th Division launched a major offensive from Cambodia into the Third Command area aimed specifically at the provincial capital of An Loc. The NVA initially attacked Loc Ninh, where the 1st ARVN Armoured Cavalry Brigade was holding defensive positions.

The ARVN unit became embroiled in some savage fighting in and around Loc Ninh, its cause being crucially supported by six Cobras from F Troop, 9th Cavalry. Flying numerous sorties over the battlefield, the AH-1 crews were responsible for eliminating a North Vietnamese PT-76 tank which was pinning down friendly troops. Hit by several 17-lb shells, the tank was initially believed to have only been damaged, but when it failed to move for more than 72 hours it was obvious that the Cobras had achieved a kill. This would be the first of several tanks destroyed by the Cobras of Task Force Garry Owen – the remaining 1st Cavalry Division assets in Vietnam.

Within a few days of the first tank engagements, old 6-lb HEAT rockets began showing up at the rearming points in Lai Khe and Song Be. These were Korean War-vintage weapons that were supposedly to be fired from fast moving jets. The warheads were removed and fitted to newer 10-lb rocket motors, which gave the 'new' HEAT rounds a very flat, high speed trajectory – deadly against tanks, but completely ineffective against surrounding targets. Also, due to their age, the early HEAT rockets experienced a rather high detonation failure rate.

However, the 'Blue Max' pilots of F/79 used these rockets to great effect in the opening hours of the armoured thrust into An Loc, which began on 13 April. 'Blue Max' AH-1s provided continuous 24-hour aerial rocket artillery support to friendly units in the besieged city.

On the morning that the An Loc offensive began, CW2 Barry McIntyre was flying as section leader, with battery commander Maj Larry McKay in his front seat, when the US advisor with the ARVN

Officers of F/9 Cav gather in front of one of their Cobras. These pilots saw extensive combat over An Loc in May 1972, defending the provincial capital from the NVA's 9th Division. WO1 Stein is standing in the centre, flanked by Capt Ron Timberlake (left) and Lt Parks, the Blue Platoon Leader (*VHPA*)

5th Division called for air support against enemy armour. The 'Blue Max' team was told to expect heavy AAA, and that the Cobras were unlikely to have any effect on the tanks. However, an attempt to even harass the armour might take the pressure off of the beleaguered ground forces. The situation on the ground was getting desperate, but when Maj McKay informed US advisor Col William H Miller that his AH-1 was equipped with HEAT rockets, things began to look up.

The 'Blue Max' Cobra flown by CW2 Ron Tusi rolled in, hitting the lead tank within metres of Col Miller's 5th ARVN Division headquarters. The enemy tanks were close enough to fire into the windows of the ARVN command post, and when the conditions further deteriorated the ground commander requested Cobras and not tactical aircraft. This was because of the proximity of friendly troops, as well as a few hapless civilians caught up in the action. The AH-1's precision was needed. CW2 Tusi responded immediately, despite intense AAA.

At one point, Tusi put himself and his Cobra in harm's way by hovering through the streets of An Loc, firing HEAT rockets at the advancing tanks. After knocking out five tanks (both T-54s and PT-76s), which caused him to run low on fuel and ammunition, he broke off his attack. Tusi's actions on that day earned him the DSC, and the honour of being F/79's first tank 'ace'.

By 15 April a new weapon had become available to the 'Blue Max' Cobras. The HEDP (High Explosive Dual Purpose) rocket was intended for anti-armour and anti-personnel missions, and was considerably more effective than the 6-lb HEAT rocket. Like the latter, it utilised a shaped-charge warhead, but the weapon also had a significant blast radius so as to allow it to eliminate soft targets. As the tank threat in An Loc dwindled, these rockets were put into use.

The NVA made one last armoured push on 24 April, but were beaten severely. The battle of An Loc had seen 'Blue Max' Cobras fly 422 combat missions. During this time they had destroyed 12 communist tanks and damaged a further six beyond repair. Twenty-five soft skinned vehicles were also destroyed, with scores more damaged. Approximately 1040 enemy troops were killed by 'Blue Max' AH-1s during the engagement, and 175 personal and crew-served weapons were captured intact. On 13 May Col Miller recommended the entire battery for the Presidential Unit Citation, stating simply, 'The Cobras were the instruments of our salvation'.

The daily journal for Third Regional Assistance Command for 6 June 1972 sums up the actions of April and May;

'Not a single Cobra had actually lost a tank engagement. Certainly, some missed their targets, but not one was destroyed by a tank, or even

Like AH-1G 67-15649, featured in the previous chapter, 'Blue Max' Cobra 67-15674 *Murder Inc* had the wiring panels for 20 mm cannon, but is shown here configured as a 'Heavy Hog', with two XM-159 19-shot rocket pods per stub wing. Photographed in early 1971, this veteran Cobra soldiered on with the 2/20th ARA until it was destroyed on 11 May 1972 defending An Loc (*Jim Moran*)

while engaging a tank. The (surface to air) missiles would prove to be more costly to the Cobras and their crews, but even they would not prevail over the attack helicopter.'

A NEW THREAT – SAMs

The NVA's thrust had initially caught the Allied forces off guard, but they were soon holding their own. In the opening weeks of the invasion, a new weapon, freshly available to NVA troops, increased the hazards of an already deadly battlefield. Initial reports of surface-to-air missile (SAM) firings near An Loc resulted in USAF but not Army helicopters being banned from the area. On 8 May a missile was fired at an F/9 Cobra flying at 2000 ft, although the weapon was logged in the unit's journal as being a B-40 unguided rocket. At low level, this would certainly have been possible, but not at 2000 ft – crews were now dealing with an entirely new threat in the form of the shoulder-launched SA-7 'Strela' SAM.

Between May and June, four Cobras were brought down by SA-7s, killing all eight crewmen. Yet despite these losses, F/79 AFA operations continued unabated.

On 21 June Capts Mike Brown and Marco Cordon were flying AH-1G 67-15725 on a mission in support of an ARVN airborne brigade south of An Loc. A total of three Cobras from F Battery had been tasked with covering the extraction of troops, one 'low bird' providing close cover for the 'slicks' and two 'high cover birds' orbiting in ideal rocket firing positions. The LZ was hot and the fire team immediately went into action. On his second firing pass, Capt Brown broke right and ran in from the south-east, before exiting the area to the north-west over Highway 13. As he was climbing back to 4000 ft to rejoin the number two Cobra, Brown's machine was struck by an SA-7. According to the pilot in his debriefing interview, the most important factor in their survival of the missile hit was that other aircraft in the area were able to observe the SAM being fired. As they observed it, they yelled, 'missile, missile, missile!' over the VHF radio.

The missile's impact completely severed the tailboom just ahead of the battery compartment. The impact was not severe, although the AH-1 began a right hand spin due to it lacking a tail rotor. Radio communication was lost, along with control of the weapons systems. Vital components of these systems were located at the root of the tailboom, and they were destroyed by the missile hit.

Using the intercom, Brown instructed his front-seater, Capt Cordon, to empty the turret weapons to lighten the load, and also to decrease the threat of explosion on impact. Cordon attempted to do so, but was unable to. Simultaneously, Brown attempted to fire out the remaining half of his rockets, but he too was unsuccessful.

Pulling complete aft cyclic and bottoming his collective pitch, Brown managed to hold a small amount of control over the spiraling Cobra. The cyclic tried to pull forward, but Brown maintained it full aft and was able to keep it against the rear stop during the entire descent. Pulling pitch at about 30 ft above the trees induced a violent spin that only stopped when the stricken Cobra hit the ground. Luckily, the trees cushioned the AH-1's impact, allowing both pilots to escape relatively unharmed.

AH-1G 68-17084 of H/17 Cavalry is seen soon after being fitted with the new SA-7 'Strela' suppression kit. The exhaust has been modified through the attachment of a 'toilet bowl' extension, which redirected engine gases up and away from the helicopter. The auxiliary intakes on the engine access panels have also been fitted with scoops to further shield the Lycoming T53-L-13 from the heat-seeking warhead of the SA-7 (*VHPA*)

Brown and Cordon were on the ground in the midst of an abandoned enemy bunker complex for roughly 15 minutes before being extracted by friendly aircraft. They both attempted to hide until a SAR helicopter made a low pass over their location, which they frantically waved down. Moments later, they were on their way back to base. Since they were the first to survive an SA-7 hit, Brown and Cordon were able to assist in the development of emergency procedures and counter-measures aimed at combating the new SAM threat.

STANDDOWN

After the NVA was beaten back, the operational tempo in-theatre dropped off considerably for the AH-1 units. In the FRAC, F/4 Cav Cobras, recently moved up to Hue-Phu Bai from Lai Khe, were tasked with escorting USMC CH-46s out to Navy ships offshore. Combat was minimal, and a sense of the war being all but over was pervasive.

August 1972 saw three Cobra units stand down and return to the US. 'Blue Max' AH-1s – one of the last two original 1st Cavalry Division units still in Vietnam – flew their last combat mission on 31 July and departed on 22 August, leaving F Troop, 9th Cav as the sole remaining 1st Cavalry unit in-country. The 361st AWC had been slated for withdrawal before the Easter invasion, and the unit also completed its return to the US in August. Finally, one of the newest Cobra units, but longest standing aviation assets in Vietnam, the 48th AHC 'Bluestars' 'slicks' and 'Jokers' AH-1s withdrew as well.

US Army helicopter operations in the autumn came to a virtual end as units prepared for the final withdrawal. The ARVN had acquitted

This aggressively marked 'Centaurs' AH-1 was one of nine Cobras flown by F/4 Cavalry from Phu Bai in late 1972. The unit was charged with covering the Marine withdrawals from Da Nang at the time (*VHPA*)

itself well during the invasion, and was now fighting without US assistance for the most part. American airpower was still employed against targets in the north, but close support helicopter assets were used sparingly. For the remainder of the year, only two Cobras were lost to enemy fire, both in isolated incidents.

1973 – ENDGAME

With the major offensives of 1972 over, and US pullout all but completed, the remaining Cobra units in-country began to stand down after New Year's Day. Limited missions were flown, except by those units escorting other aerial assets to coastal areas for the pullout.

The AH-1 units that remained in South Vietnam fell under the control of, from north to south, the 11th Combat Aviation Group in Da Nang (comprising F/4th Cav, D/17th Cav and H/17th Cav), the 17th Aviation Group at Pleiku (57th AHC, 60th AHC and 129th AHC), the 12th Aviation Group at Bien Hoa (F/8th Cav) and the 164th Aviation Group (C/16th Cav) in Can Tho. Each of these units maintained combat capability, and they continued to conduct missions in support of ARVN units throughout the country. It was clear, however, that the American presence was dwindling rapidly, and pullout was imminent.

The 'Blue Ghosts' of F Troop, 8th Cavalry had moved south to Bien Hoa and been attached to the 12th Aviation Group in the latter half of 1972. President Nixon announced the cessation of offensive operations against North Vietnam on 15 January 1973, and this same day F/8 Cav lost its final Cobra when AH-1G 68-15055 was destroyed in an operational accident – no casualties were reported.

The next day, H Troop, 17th Cav lost the final Cobra of the war to another operational accident. The AH-1 in question had just returned from a mission and landed at the Da Nang refuelling point. WO1 Phillips, the aircraft commander, exited the Cobra and began refuelling. When the helicopter's tanks showed that 1350 lbs of fuel was on board, Phillips attempted to release the nozzle, which jammed. The fuel shutoff valve failed, and when the pilot was able to remove the nozzle,

AH-1G 68-17074 *the GLADIATOR*, flown by WO1 Dan Shaver, departs Can Tho airfield in late 1972. C/16 Cav was the last Cobra unit to serve in IV Corps, and the men and aircraft of the 'Darkhorse' Troop flew combat missions right up to the ceasefire. This particular Cobra had previously seen service with the 5th Aviation Detachment at Vung Tau prior to it being assigned to C Troop, 16th Cavalry in late 1971. This was the second C/16 AH-1G to feature the name *the GLADIATOR*, this aircraft continuing a tradition started with 66-15328. Like '074, '328 was also a 20 mm cannon-equipped Cobra (*Gary Gardina*)

WO1 Ron Paye of the 129th AHC poses at An Son with a carefully arranged display of the firepower carried by the Cobra in Vietnam. The 129th was one of the last four units to convert to the AH-1G in Vietnam, all of which were based in II Corps. The 'King Cobras' had between four and six AH-1Gs assigned to the platoon from January 1972 through to the ceasefire in January 1973. It eventually returned to the US on 13 March that same year (*Ron Paye*)

fuel was then sucked into the intake, causing a fire that completely destroyed the aircraft. Both crewmen were able to get away from the aircraft without injury.

The rest of the month was spent preparing units for their return home. The remaining air cav units in Vietnam rotated back to the US on 26 February, followed by the 57th 'Cougars', 60th 'Ghost Riders' and 129th 'King Cobras' on 13 March.

At peak strength, there were nearly 700 AH-1Gs operating in South Vietnam, but by the beginning of February 1973, that number had dwindled to just 63.

The Cobra's combat experience in Vietnam had thoroughly proved that the attack helicopter had a place on the modern battlefield. The operational testing of the type exceeded all expectations, and Bell's production line met the US Army's challenge by supplying hundreds of AH-1s in a very short period of time. The gestation period for the Cobra was remarkably short for a modern combat aircraft, Bell and the US Army moving from concept design and theoretical application to an operational combat aircraft in less than two years.

Operating the AH-1G tasked the pilots with not only learning a new aircraft, but also creating completely new tactics. The Cobra allowed greater firepower and flexibility than any previous weapons platform, and proved that the attack helicopter could more than handle both the close air support and armed reconnaissance missions. Development for future variants was guaranteed with the introduction of the TOW system in 1972, which would make the Cobra the Army's ultimate 'tank-killer' in the years to come.

A 'Blue Max' Cobra flies over South Vietnam at altitude just prior to the unit's return to the US (*Jim Moran*)

APPENDICES

APPENDIX A

UNITS BY CORPS, CALLSIGN AND NUMBER OF AIRCRAFT AUTHORISED

I CORPS

	Callsign	Cobras Authorised
48th AHC	'Joker'	4
173rd AHC	'Crossbow'	4
D/101st AHB, 101st Abn	'Hawk'	12
D/158th AHB, 101st Abn	'Redskin'	12
2/17th Cav, 101st Abn		
A Troop	'Assault'	9
B Troop	'Banshee'	9
C Troop	'Condor'	9
4/77th ARA, 101st Abn		
A Battery	'Dragon'	12
B Battery	'Toro'	12
C Battery	'Griffin'	12
B/123rd Abn	'Warlord'	6
F/8th Cav	'Blue Ghost'	9
D/1/1st Cav	'Sword'	9

II CORPS

	Callsign	Cobras Authorised
B/4th Abn, 4th ID	'Gambler Guns'	6
D/2/1st Cav	'Blackhawk'	9
D/1/10th Cav	'Sabre'	9
7/17th Cav	'Ruthless Rider'	
A Troop	'Knight'	9
B Troop	'Undertaker'	9
C Troop	'Yellow Scarf'	9
361st AWC	'Panther'	12
238th AWC	'Gunrunner'	12
57th AHC	'Cougar'	4
60th AHC	'Ghostrider'	6
129th AHC	'King Cobra'	4

III CORPS

	Callsign	Cobras Authorised
B/1st Abn, 1st ID	'Rebel'	6
D/1/4th Cav 1st ID	'Darkhorse'	9
B/25th Abn	'Diamondhead'	6
D/3/4th Cav, 25th ID	'Centaur'	9
334th AHC	'Sabre'	
1st Platoon	'Playboy'	6
2nd Platoon	'Raider'	6
3rd Platoon	'Dragon'	6
3/17th Cav	'Redhorse'	
A Troop	'Silver Spur'	9
B Troop	'Burning Stogie'	9
C Troop	'Charliehorse'	9
D/227th AHB	'El Lobo'	12
D/229th AHB	'Smiling Tiger'	12
2/20th ARA	'Blue Max'	
A Battery		12
B Battery		12
C Battery (later F/79th AFA)		12
1/9th Cav	'Bullwhip'	

	Callsign	Cobras Authorised
A Troop	'Apache'	9
B Troop	'Bravo'	9
C Troop	'Cavalier'	9
ACT/11	'Thunderhorse'	9
187th AHC	'Rat Pack'	6

IV CORPS

	Callsign	Cobras Authorised
7/1st Cav	'Blackhawk'	
A Troop	'Apache'	9
B Troop	'Dutchmaster'	9
C Troop	'Comanche'	9
235th AWC	'Delta Devil'	
1st Platoon	'Satan'	8
2nd Platoon	'Death Dealer'	8
3rd Platoon	'Viper'	8
C/16th Cav	'Darkhorse'	9
D/3/5th Cav	'Crusader'	9
B/9th Avn	'Stingray'	6
114th AHC	'Cobra'	6

APPENDIX B

COBRA LOSSES BY YEAR

1967	0
1968	23
1969	78
1970	78
1971	68
1972	30
1973	2

Total – 279 (all causes)

APPENDIX C

AH-1G PRODUCTION BLOCKS BY CONTRACT YEAR

1966	66-15249 – 66-15357
1967	67-15450 – 67-15869
1968	68-15000 – 68-15213
1968	68-17020 – 68-17113
1969	69-16410 – 69-16447
1970	70-15936 – 70-16105
1971	71-20983 – 71-21052

APPENDIX D

WEAPONS SYSTEMS

TAT-102A Turret – single M-134 Minigun (GAU-2B/A)

M-28A1 Turret – minigun (GAU-2B/A) and 40 mm grenade launcher (M-129)

XM-18 – Minigun pod with 1500 rounds

XM-157 – rocket pod (seven-shot), non-removable tubes

XM-158 – rocket pod (seven-shot), removable tubes

XM-159 – rocket pod (19-shot), removable tubes

XM-200 – rocket pod (19-shot), non-removable tubes

XM-35 – 20 mm M-195 cannon mounted under left wing stub

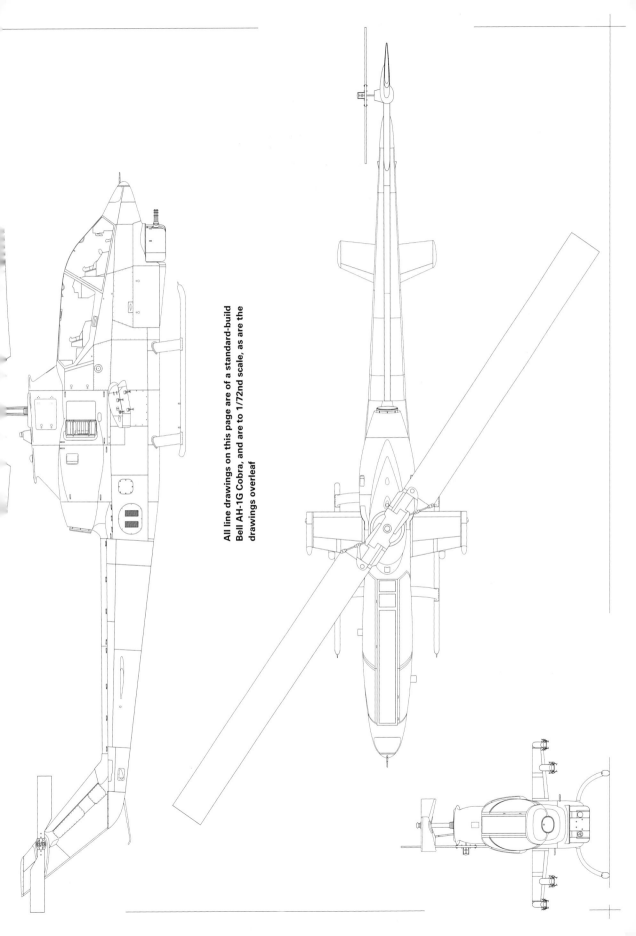

All line drawings on this page are of a standard-build
Bell AH-1G Cobra, and are to 1/72nd scale, as are the
drawings overleaf

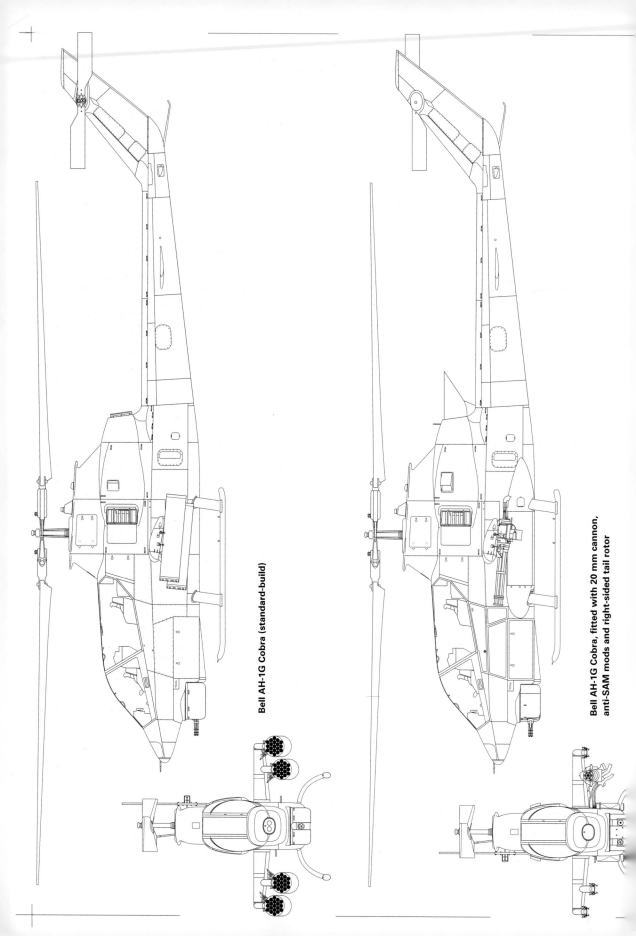

Bell AH-1G Cobra (standard-build)

Bell AH-1G Cobra, fitted with 20 mm cannon, anti-SAM mods and right-sided tail rotor

COLOUR PLATES

1
AH-1G 66-15259 *"Virginia Rose II"* of Cobra NETT, flown by Col Paul Anderson (aircraft commander) and Maj Nicolas P Stein, Bien Hoa, September 1967

This Cobra completed the first in-country flight for the type in South Vietnam on 4 September 1967. Its unusual camouflage scheme was derived from USAF paint stocks held at Bien Hoa, and 66-15259 was one of two AH-1s used by Cobra NETT to feature this white/tan/olive finish.

2
AH-1G 66-15263 of Cobra NETT, flown by WO1 John D Thomson (aircraft commander) and Gen George Seneff, Muc Hoa, 8 September 1967

Gen George Seneff, commander of the 1st Aviation Brigade, had his Cobra orientation flight in this more conventionally camouflaged machine cut short on 8 September 1967 when he and WO1 J D Thomson spotted an unattended sampan in a free-fire zone. The crew rolled in and duly scored the first combat kills to be attributed to the Cobra.

3
AH-1G 66-15272 of the 334th AHC, flown by Capt Ken Rubin (aircraft commander) and SP4 Jessie Robertson, Bien Hoa, 16 November 1967

This aircraft was the first Cobra 'downed' by hostile fire, the helicopter being hit at least five times my 0.30-cal machine gun rounds on 16 November 1967. A single bullet damaged an electrical line, which in turn caused the illumination of a warning light on Capt Rubin's control panel. Instead of risking the aircraft, he set it down, and the AH-1 was subsequently sling-loaded under a CH-47 and returned to base. 66-15272 was eventually destroyed on 4 August 1969 while operating with the 4th Aviation Battalion. As a rule, AH-1s did not have assigned front-seaters/gunners in South Vietnam, aircraft commanders instead pairing up with newly arrived pilots who rotated through front seat duty until they themselves became aircraft commanders after about four months in-country, or 300 hours of combat time.

4
AH-1G 67-15464 of B/7/1 Cav, flown by WO1 Len Constantine (aircraft commander) and SP5 Russell Stewart as Crew Chief, Vinh Long, Autumn 1968

Based at Vinh Long, in IV Corps, this aircraft was heavily involved in Operation *Blackhawk* (an offensive launched in late 1968 that was designed to place round-the-clock pressure on NVA and VC infiltration routes along the Cambodian border), providing fire support for US 9th Division elements and ARVN ground units. 7/1 Cav was tasked with flying both day and night sorties in order to keep a constant watch for enemy movement along the Cambodian border. An ex-334th AHC machine,

67-15464 was eventually destroyed on 6 March 1971 whilst on an armed reconnaissance mission during *Lam Son 719* (the invasion of Laos, which commenced on 29 January 1971).

5
AH-1G 67-15460 of C/7/1 Cav, flown by CW2 Damon 'Cec' Cecil (aircraft commander), Muc Hoa, Spring 1969

CW2 Cecil flew this Cobra as part of 'Comanche' Troop in support of elements of the 9th Infantry Division in the Mekong Delta during Operation *Blackhawk* in early 1969. He and an unnamed gunner had a close escape in this very machine when, on one of the offensive's early night flights, he nearly impacted the ground when a flare was dropped close to the AH-1, blinding Cecil. Having just managed to recover the aircraft, he then nearly collided with a spent flare canister whilst attempting to regain height. The use of flares in conjunction with low level gunship operations was discontinued shortly thereafter.

6
AH-1G 67-15651 of C/7/17 Cav, flown by 1Lt Sterling Cox (aircraft commander) and WO1 James Petteys, Plei Djereng, 15 January 1969

On 15 January 1969, this 'Yellow Scarf' 'Pink Team' Cobra was brought down by heavy calibre machine gun fire near Plei Djereng, in II Corps. Its pilot, 1Lt Sterling Cox, tried to recover the AH-1, but in its rapid descent, the helicopter hit high trees and exploded. Both Cox and WO1 James Petteys were killed instantly. During the subsequent r escue mission by the troop's aero-rifle platoon to retrieve the bodies of the crew, PFC Garfield Langhorn smothered an enemy grenade whilst protecting other wounded soldiers, thus earning himself a posthumous Medal of Honor.

7
AH-1G 67-15815 *HAPPINESS IS A WARM GUN* of the B/9th Avn Bn, flown by Capt Robert Schultz (aircraft commander), Dong Tam, February 1969

This AH-1, assigned to the CO of B/9 Avn Bn, carries the stencilled message *HAPPINESS IS A WARM GUN* on its ammunition bay door. Following the 9th Division's departure from Vietnam in August 1969, the Cobra was assigned to B Troop, 3/17 Cavalry, and it remained in-country until mid-1972, when it too returned to the US. Although only in existence as a Cobra unit for six months, the 'Stingrays' of B Company had closely supported 9th Division ground assets. B/9, led by Capt Robert Schultz, had been one of few gunship companies to work in |conjunction with the Mobile Riverine Force operating in IV Corps. Hunting VC/NVA sampans in the Mekong Delta, the 'Stingrays' acquitted themselves admirably in actions around Dong Tam in late December 1968.

89

8
AH-1G 67-15??? *VooDo LADY* of the 11th ACR (crew unknown), Daub Ting, April 1969

Operating with the callsign 'Thunderhorse', the Air Cav Troop of the 11th ACR received its Cobras in the summer of 1968, and remained in Vietnam with these machines until early 1972. This aircraft (whose serial is unknown) saw action during Operation *Atlas Wedge* in April 1969, 11th ACR AH-1s flying closely in support of the 1st Infantry Division and the 11th Armored Cavalry Division. Both units had caught a large contingent of bicycle-mounted NVA troops in the open in the Michelin Rubber Plantation in III Corps, and *Atlas Wedge* was rapidly launched in order to eliminate this force.

9
AH-1G 67-15698 of A/2/17 Cav, flown by CW2 Len Constantine (aircraft commander), A Shau Valley, RVN, 14 May 1969

Of the countless interesting and unusual engagements of the Vietnam War, CW2 Len Constantine's encounter with a MiG-21 stands out as unique. Although his (unknown) gunner succeeded in damaging the MiG with the Cobra's GAU-2B machine gun, any claim for a confirmed kill proved to be impossible. 67-15698 was brought down by enemy fire and destroyed on 18 February 1971.

10
AH-1G 68-15139 *SQUATTER SWATTER* of D/1/4 Cav, flown by 1Lt Dean Sinor (aircraft commander), Daub Ting, June 1969

AH-1G 68-15139 was the second Cobra to wear the *SQUATTER SWATTER* nose art, this particular helicopter being issued to D Troop in July 1969 as an attrition replacement machine. Serving with the unit until the division's withdrawal in March 1970, 68-15139, along with assets of the 1st Aviation Battalion and the remainder of D Troop 1/4th Cav, was turned over to the newly organised C Troop 16th Cav and moved south to Can Tho, in IV Corps.

11
AH-1G 68-15146 of the B/25th Avn Bn, flown by CW2 Greg Bucy (aircraft commander) and SP4 Robert Michaels, Cu Chi, August 1969

Boasting a fearsome sharksmouth, this Cobra survived the war and was later converted into an AH-1S – one of 198 AH-1Gs upgraded during the late 1970s. The combat veteran is now resident in the American Airpower Heritage Museum in Midland, Texas.

12
AH-1G 67-15686 *DDAP* of D/1/1 Cav, flown by Capt Mike Henry (aircraft commander) and Capt Leo Huber, Chu Lai, 16 May 1969

This Cobra, flying as 'Sword 75', took multiple 0.51-cal machine gun hits whilst conducting a reconnaissance sweep near Chu Lai. Although gunner Capt Leo Huber was killed and aircraft commander Capt Mike Henry wounded in the left leg and right hand, the AH-1 stayed aloft, allowing the pilot to keep the helicopter under control and perform a running landing back at Tam Ky. The Cobra was eventually returned to combat duty, but was destroyed by enemy fire on 15 February 1970 (both crewmen were injured). The yellow *DDAP* script below the pilot's cockpit stands for 'Dead Dinks Are Pacified', which was a satirical commentary by GIs on the post-1968 'pacification' programme initiated in South Vietnam by Military Assistance Command Vietnam.

13
AH-1G 67-15816 *SATAN 10* of the 1st Platoon, 235th AWC, flown by WO1 Roscoe Armstrong (aircraft commander), Can Tho, November 1969

Depicted here after a recent respray in the autumn of 1969, this Cobra had seen extensive combat with the 235th since its arrival in-country in late 1968, and had been damaged on no less than ten separate occasions. The landing lights fitted in the helicopter's nose had been removed by this point, and the titling *SATAN 10* painted inside the empty nose cap. Having survived so many close shaves in combat, 67-15816 was finally destroyed when it crashed during a seemingly routine ferry flight on 11 September 1971 while serving with the 361st AWC.

14
AH-1G 67-15762 *EXECUTIONER* of the 235th AC, flown by Capt Lou Bouault (aircraft commander) Daub Ting, November 1969

Capt Bouault (formerly company commander of B/1st Aviation Battalion, dubbed the 'Rebels') often flew missions from the front seat of this Cobra during his tenure as 'Rebel 6'. Although a qualified AH-1 aircraft commander, Bouault preferred to control the mission, rather than becoming preoccupied with fighting, and flying, in a single helicopter. Indeed, he duly rebuilt the 235th AC in the spring of 1970 after he was made company commander, changing the unit's AH-1 tactics by emphasising low-level attack flying just a few feet off the ground. Such missions quickly boosted the morale of the troops both in the air and on the ground. Previously, the unit had been held back by a minimum altitude restriction, which negated the Cobra's ability to accurately place rocket fire in support of friendly troops.

15
AH-1G 67-15865 *BLUE GHOST* of F/8th Cav, flown by Capt Robert Wiggins (aircraft commander), Tam Ky, January 1970

Capt Wiggins was at the controls of this machine when it was shot down by 0.51-cal fire on 6 January 1970 while defending the firebase at LZ Baldy, which was being overrun. 67-15865 had been Wiggins' aircraft for much of his tour in Vietnam, including the 25 November 1969 mission that had seen him awarded the DFC. The Cobra was repaired following the crash and issued to D Troop, 2/1 Cav in April 1970.

16
AH-1G 67-15838 of A/4/77 ARA, flown by WO1 Robert Sullivan (aircraft commander) and WO1 Tom Damm, Camp Evans, February 1970
This Cobra suffered an engine failure while on a visual reconnaissance mission near the Razorback area of I Corps. It was one of the few AH-1s in the 4/77th to have twin miniguns installed in the turret. The M-28 turret replaced the original Emerson TAT-102A in-theatre from mid 1968, the system being retro-fitted to older Cobras in the frontline by Army groundcrews. The M-28 featured both a 40 mm M-129 automatic grenade launcher (right) and an M-134 7.62 mm minigun (left), the new turret being able to accept one of each weapon or two of one type. Due to the scarcity of the M-129's installation hardware, dual grenade launcher configurations were rarely seen. However, dual minigun turrets became more common as the war progressed.

17
AH-1G 68-17051 'White 67' of C/2/20 ARA, flown by CW2 Paul Garrity (aircraft commander) and WO1 Jim Nabours, Quan Loi, 24 May 1970
For CW2 Paul Garrity and WO1 Jim Nabours, flying 68-17051, the 24 May 1970 mission covering UH-1 'Medevac 2' began as a routine extraction of wounded ARVN personnel in a supposedly cold LZ in Cambodia. Operating as 'Precise Swords 12A', they were providing high cover for the flight in this AH-1G when withering fire erupted from the treeline, downing 'Medevac 2'. Garrity rolled in and began placing rockets on the camouflaged bunkers spotted in the surrounding treeline, making numerous passes until his ammunition was expended. The survivors of the shot down Huey remained surrounded on the ground until the following morning, when they were finally lifted out to safety. Virtually all of C Battery's 12 AH-1s saw action in support of this rescue.

18
AH-1G 68-15049 'White R1' of C/2/20 ARA, flown by 1Lt George Alexander (aircraft commander) and WO1 Jim Moran, Bu Dop, June 1970
Flying as 'Romeo 1' on the 24 May 1970 Medal of Honor mission depicted in Mark Postlethwaite's specially commissioned cover artwork for this volume, AH-1G 68-15049 suffered numerous 0.30- and 0.51-cal machine gun hits prior to 1Lt Alexander and WO1 Moran departing the area, their ammunition exhausted. The Cobra was repaired and flying again by the next day. The radio compartment hatch on the non-standard black tailboom was scavenged as a replacement from another Cobra, hence its Olive Drab colouring and letters 'ATE' from the UNITED STATES ARMY titling, present on the donor AH-1. The black paint on the tailboom on 69-15049 was hastily applied in order to obscure any US markings on helicopters participating in the Cambodian invasion. According to Jim Moran, 'someone at higher headquarters got the bright idea to paint out the national insignia, so

if anyone on the ground saw us they "wouldn't know who we were" – like anyone else was operating helicopters in South Vietnam and Cambodia!' B Battery 2/20 ARA also flew an all black Cobra at around this time too.

19
AH-1G 66-15262 *HULK* of D/227 AHB, flown by WO1 John A Henry (aircraft commander), Phuoc Vinh June 1970
Although this was one of the first Cobras to arrive in Vietnam, by the time of its participation in the invasion of Cambodia (launched on 29 April 1970) 66-15262 had been refitted with an M-28 turret in place of the original Emerson TAT-102A system. *HULK* was one of several colourfully marked 'El Lobo' AH-1s to participate in the Cambodian invasion.

20
AH-1G 68-15062 *THE CRYSTAL SHIP* of C/1/9 Cav, flown by CW2 Walker Jones (aircraft commander) and SP4 'Mac' McCloy as Crew Chief, Phuoc Vinh, May 1970
Walker Jones flew this aircraft on numerous occasions up until March 1971, when it was destroyed by 0.51-cal machine gun fire during a combat mission while he was on R&R. It was being flown by 1Lt Van Joyce and gunner Capt Joel Hageman at the time of its demise, both of whom were killed when it was shot down.

21
AH-1G 68-17068 *CINDY ANN* of C/1/9 Cav, flown by CW2 Randy Zahn (aircraft commander) and SP4 Marshall Maring as Crew Chief, Phuoc Vinh, August 1970
This helicopter, along with AH-1 69-16437 (see profile 21), were the two 20 mm cannon-equipped Cobras assigned to C Troop in 1970. To augment the firepower of the 20 mm weapon, twin miniguns were also carried in the turret as well. The cut-down 20 mm M-61 Vulcan cannon (known as the M-195 when fitted to the AH-1) was de-rated to fire 750 rpm, with ammunition fed via two canisters attached to either side of the fuselage above the skids. Each of these held 950 rounds, as well as the associated crossover ammunition feed chutes. The flat trajectory and long range of the M-195 at last gave Cobra crews a chance to hit back at the NVA's 0.51-cal AAA positions, whilst at the same time remaining out of range of the previously deadly heavy machine gun.

22
AH-1G 69-16437 *Heather Dawn* of C/1/9 Cav, flown by Capt John Craig (aircraft commander), Phuoc Vinh, June 1970
Also boasting the M-195 cannon modification, 69-16437 was originally christened *'Betty K'*. However, John Craig renamed the AH-1 when he became aircraft commander in June 1970. *Heather Dawn* saw extensive combat in Cambodia throughout June 1970, and remained with the 1st

Cavalry Division until June of the following year, when it was one of the first Cobras assigned to the 173rd AHC at Da Nang. This machine survived the war, and is now an exhibit in the New Jersey Aviation Hall of Fame.

23

AH-1G 69-16439 of A/3/17 Cav, flown by CW2 Dave Tela (aircraft commander), Di An, June 1970
Flown by DFC-winner Dave Tela, AH-1 69-16439 was yet another 20 mm cannon-modified Cobra that saw extensive combat in Cambodia in May-June 1970. It was reassigned to C/2/17 Cav in June 1971 and then F/4 Cav in early 1972, before finally returning to the US after the ceasefire. Configured as a 'super scout', 69-16439 carried three XM-158 seven-shot rocket pods along with the 20 mm cannon.

24

AH-1G 68-15209 'White 30' *V.C. BIRTH CONTROL* of the 114th AHC, flown by CW2 Bob Baker (aircraft commander), Vinh Long, 1970
Adorned with an elaborate Cobra artwork and poignant nickname, 68-15209 was flown by CW2 Baker during the assault on Phu Quoc Island in the late summer of 1970, when the 114th AHC hit a major VC/NVA Rest & Recreation camp off the western IV Corps Coast.

25

AH-1G 68-15074 *Dr Pepper/Kill/RAT PACK* of the 187th AHC, flown by Capt Carl Key (aircraft commander), Tay Ninh, September 1970
This particular AH-1 was the first right-hand tail rotored Cobra assigned to the 187th, the blade switch greatly increasing the pilot's control of the Cobra at low speed, high power/high torque settings.

26

AH-1G 68-15531 *the Magical Mystery tour* of D/229 AWC, flown by 1Lt Roger Fox (aircraft commander), Quan Loi, 1971
Adorned with the titling *the Magical Mystery tour* atop a green three-leafed clover, as well as a 'Smiling Tigers' badge, 68-15531 was transferred to D/229th during the reorganisation of the 3rd Airmobile Brigade in the spring of 1971. It flew with the unit until it was destroyed in-theatre in August 1972.

27

AH-1G 68-17054 *Sound of Silence* of C/2/20 ARA, flown by CW2 Jim Moran (aircraft commander) and WO1 Neil MacMillan, LZ Mace, January 1971
Jim Moran was flying this Cobra on the LRRP extraction mission on 21 January 1971 that saw him recommended for a Silver Star. Although slated to DEROS (Date of Expected Return from OverSeas) within the next few days, Moran accepted the mission and maintained control of an increasingly dangerous situation at night, and in bad weather, and got the LRRP team out safely.

28

AH-1G 68-15002 of D/158 AHB, flown by CW2 Donald Wann (aircraft commander) and 1Lt Paul Magers, Khe Sanh, February
This Cobra was lost on a LRRP extraction mission on 1 June 1971, the reconnaissance team being successfully recovered by 'slicks' protected by AH-1s from D/158 AHB. CW2 Wann was then instructed to destroy a weapons cache that had been discovered by the LRRP team, and as the Cobra commenced its firing pass, it was hit in the underside by several heavy calibre machine gun rounds. The AH-1 was then seen to rear up, before spiralling down into a hillside below and exploding on impact. Neither Wann or Magers survived.

29

AH-1G 68-15031 *Pandora's Box* of the 238th AWC, flown by CW2 Gene Kennedy (aircraft commander), Pleiku, June 1971
The 238th acquired 12 Cobras in June 1971 and quickly initiated operations (typically convoy escort and standing alert in support of ARVN infantry) in II Corps. This aircraft flew with B/2/20 ARA until the Cav left Vietnam in April 1971. 68-15031 remained with the 238th through to December of that year, when it became part of the newly formed 60th AHC.

30

AH-1G 68-15207 of the 175th AHC, flown by Capt Harris (aircraft commander) and SP4 Jim Stanley, Vinh Long, Summer 1971
68-15207 was the first 20 mm cannon-equipped Cobra to be issued to the 175th 'Bushwackers' after the unit transitioned to the AH-1 in the summer of 1971. The company further augmented an already large Cobra presence at Vinh Long, and conducted operations with the AH-1 until February 1972.

31

AH-1G 68-17074 *the GLADIATOR* of C/16 Cav, flown by WO1 Dan E Shaver (aircraft commander), Can Tho, January 1972
This Cobra had previously seen service with the 5th Aviation Detachment at Vung Tau prior to it being assigned to C Troop, 16th Cavalry in late 1971. This was the second C/16 AH-1 to feature the name *the GLADIATOR*, the aircraft continuing a tradition started with 66-15328. Like '074, '328 was also a 20 mm cannon-equipped Cobra.

32

AH-1G 68-15012 *#1 DU M̲E̲ MI* of F/4 Cav, flown by CW2 Ken Mick (aircraft commander), Hue-Phu Bai, late 1972
The advent of the shoulder-launched, heat-seeking SA-7 'Strela' SAM posed such a threat to all helicopters in 1972 that US forces hastily initiated a series of modifications to increase the survivability of their aircraft in South Vietnam. With the AH-1, these 'mods' took the form of a 'toilet bowl' exhaust and auxiliary scoops on the engine intakes

in order to mask the heat signature generated by the engine from the SA-7. By mid-1972 priority was given to retrofitting 'Strela' suppression kits to all combat helicopters. The garishly decorated AH-1 68-15012 was amongst the first Cobras to receive the suppression kit.

33
AH-1G 68-15053 of the 361st AWC, flown by Capt Bill Reeder (aircraft commander) and 1Lt Tim Conry, Camp Holloway, Pleiku, 9 May 1972
Capt Reeder was leading an armed escort mission covering 'slicks' from the 57th AHC near the tri-border region of II Corps in this Cobra when it received several hits to its engine and started to go down. The AH-1 crashed and burned, and both crewmen broke their backs in the impact with the ground. Lt Conry made it out of the wreckage, but soon died of his wounds in an OH-6 whilst on his way to hospital. Capt Reeder also attempted to escape the flaming helicopter, but he got stuck when his survival vest hung up on the seat armour, suspending him inverted outside the aircraft. Struggling to get free, Reeder was finally thrown clear of the wrecked AH-1 when flames reached the helicopter's fuel tank and it exploded. The pilot was captured by NVA forces three days later, and he duly spent nine months in a North Vietnamese prison before being released in March 1973.

34
AH-1G 67-15725 of F/79 AFA, flown by Capt Mike Brown (aircraft commander) and Capt Marco Cordon, An Loc, 21 June 1972
Relying on his excellent training and piloting skills, Capt Mike Brown managed to maintain enough control of this Cobra after taking a direct SA-7 hit (the missile completely severed the aircraft's tailboom) to allow both himself and his front-seater to survive the inevitable crash. Prior to this incident, no helicopter crew had survived a SAM strike. The lessons learned from this incident allowed American helicopter units to adapt to the new threat, and create effective countermeasures in order to negate it.

35
AH-1G 68-15101 of H/10 Cav (crew unknown), Pleiku, Autumn 1972
C Troop, 7/17 Cavalry was redesignated H Troop 10th Cavalry in April 1972 when the remainder of the 'Ruthless Riders' were sent back to the US. Well-weathered 68-15101 was one of 27 AH-1s on strength at the time of the redesignation, the helicopter boasting the unit's subtly-applied 'stars & stripes' at the base of the tail unit. H Troop, 10th Cavalry operated in II Corps until the ceasefire in January 1973.

36
AH-1G 67-15738 of the 129th AHC, flown by CW2 Ron Paye (aircraft commander), An Son, Summer 1972

The 129th AHC was one of the last four units to convert to the AH-1 in Vietnam, all of which were based in II Corps. The 'King Cobras' had between four and six AH-1s assigned to the platoon from January 1972 through to the ceasefire in January 1973. The 129th eventually returned to the US on 13 March that same year.

COLOUR SECTION

1, 2 & 3
Literally hundreds of Cobras were delivered to South-East Asia by sea, this sequence of photographs showing a deck full of AH-1Gs aboard the USS *Point Cruz* soon after the fast transport carrier's arrival off South Vietnam sometime in 1969. The aircraft were 'wrapped' in protective canvas bags for the sea crossing, these in turn being removed once the ex-World War 2 escort carrier had docked in South Vietnam. The helicopters were assembled aboard ship and their engines run (but no armament fitted), before being flown off to their combat units. Other types visible 'under wraps' in these photos include CH-46 Sea Knights, OV-10 Broncos and OV-1 Mohawks – the latter fixed-wing types were craned off the carrier (*Bell via Mike Verier*)

4
A rear view of the awesome XM-35 gun system fitted to the AH-1G. This weapon was developed for the Cobra following pressure from Dick Jarrett's NETT unit in Vietnam. Based on the 20 mm Vulcan rotary cannon, the whole system weighed nearly 1200 lbs, but it gave the Cobra a considerable increase in effective range and killing power when dealing with heavy calibre 0.30- and 0.51-cal machine guns (*Bell via Mike Verier*)

5
Something of a mystery machine, this two-tone camouflaged AH-1G carries what appears to be the 'Blue Max' emblem on its rotor gear housing. Flown here by a single crewman, the Cobra, and its unit allocation, remain unclear (*Bell via Mike Verier*)

6
'Devil's Tower' – the 'personalised' water tower which served the 235th AWC 'Delta Devils'' compound at Can Tho Army Airfield (*Roscoe Armstrong*)

7
AH-1G 67-15816 *SATAN 10* of the 1st Platoon, 235th AWC, flown by WO1 Roscoe Armstrong (aircraft commander), was photographed at Can Tho in the autumn of 1969. The wear and tear inflicted on Cobras during their near daily low-level combat sorties in all kinds of weather is readily apparent here – '816 was resprayed shortly after

this shot was taken. Note the *SATAN 10* titling in place of the nose landing lights (*Roscoe Armstrong*)

8

Parked within their own individual blast revetments at Bien Hoa, these brand new 'Playboy' Platoon AH-1Gs were photographed in the autumn of 1967 by Cobra NETT crew chief SP4 Jessie Robertson. He was working on the tail rotor of the machine in the foreground at the time – note the rotor blade lent against the revetment wall (*Jessie Robertson*)

9

235th AWC AH-1s dominate the flightline at Can Tho Army Air Field in late 1969. Parked behind the Cobras are a mixed fleet of UH-1C/Hs (*Roscoe Armstrong*)

10

A C Troop, 3/17th Cavalry AH-1G undergoes major engine maintenance at Phu Loi in 1970. Cobra crew chiefs maintained their helicopters when in the frontline, but major overhauls and inspections were conducted by maintenance units at larger bases further to the 'rear', such as Phu Loi (*Author's collection*)

11

AH-1G 68-15089 of C Battery, 2/20 ARA cruises over jungle near Bu Dop during the summer of 1970. Clear blue skies and excellent visibility were a rarity in Vietnam (*Jim Moran*)

12

Nicknamed *THE WIDOW MAKER*, this sharksmouthed (but now weaponless) AH-1G saw extensive combat with D Troop, 1/4th Cavalry during Operation *Atlas Wedge*. It is seen here at Phu Loi undergoing much-needed maintenance in the aftermath of the campaign (*Author's collection*)

13

AH-1G 68-15049 'Romeo 1' was the Cobra flown by Lt George Alexander and WO1 Jim Moran on the on 24 May 1970 'Medevac Meadow' Medal of Honor-winning mission (*Jim Moran*)

14

'Charliehorse' AH-1G 67-15591 of C/3/17 is serviced between sorties at the unit's Di An base in the autumn of 1969. This aircraft arrived in Vietnam in July 1968 and was eventually destroyed on 9 August 1970. Note the CH-47 parked to the right of the Cobra (*Author's collection*)

15

Another view of the extensive maintenance facilities at Phu Loi, which serviced all manner of US Army helicopter types in-theatre for much of the Vietnam campaign. In the background is AH-1G 68-15152 from A battery, 2/20 ARA, while at the right is an OH-6A Cayuse, or 'Loach', undergoing a rotor blade change (*Author's collection*)

BIBLIOGRAPHY

Books

BOYLE, JEROME M, *Apache Sunrise, Ivy Books, New York, 1994*
DRENDEL, LOU, *Gunslingers in Action, Aircraft Vol 14 Squadron/Signal Publications, Carrolton, Texas, 1974*
ERICSON, DON, AND JOHN L ROTUNDO, *Charlie Rangers Ivy Books. New York, 1989*
HOBSON, CHRIS, *Vietnam Air Losses, Midland Publishing, Hinckley, England, 2001*
MARVICSIN, DENNIS, *MAVERICK - The personal war of a Vietnam Cobra pilot, Putnam. New York, 1990*
MUTZA, WAYNE, *AH-1 Cobra in Action; Aircraft Vol 168 Squadron/Signal Publications, Carrolton, Texas, 1998*
MUTZA, WAYNE, *Walk Around, AH-1 Cobra; Walk Around No 29 Squadron/Signal Publications, Carrolton, Texas, 2002*
NOLAN, KEITH WILLIAM, *Death Valley: The Summer Offensive for I Corps, August 1969, Presidio Press, Novato, California, 1999*
NOLAN, KEITH WILLIAM, *Into Cambodia*
NOLAN, KEITH WILLIAM, *Into Laos*
NOLAN, KEITH WILLIAM, *The Battle for Saigon, Tet, 1968 Presidio Press, Novato, California, 2002*
PEACOCK, LINDSAY, *AH-1 HueyCobra, Osprey, London, 1987*
PEOPLES, KENNETH, *Aerofax Datagraph 4: Bell AH-1 Cobra Variants, Aerofax Publishing, Inc, Arlington, Texas, 1988*
PLASTER, JOHN L, *SOG, Simon & Schuster. New York, 1997*
SHAWCROSS, WILLIAM, *Sideshow: Kissinger, Nixon and the Destruction of Cambodia, Simon & Schuster. New York, 1997*
SORLEY, LEWIS, *A Better War, Harcourt & Brace, New York, 1999*
SPAULDING, RICHARD D, *Centaur Flights, Ivy Books. New York, 1996*
STANTON, SHELBY, *Anatomy of a Division: 1st Cav In Vietnam, Presidio Press, Novato, California, 1987*
STANTON, SHELBY, *Vietnam Order of Battle, Galahad Books, New York, 1987*
VERIER, MIKE, *Osprey Air Combat – Bell AH-1 Cobra, Osprey, London, 1990*

Contributing Websites:

http://vhfcn.org/unitlinks.html
http://www.vhpa.org
http://www.vhpamuseum.org
http://members.aol.com/bear317/spurs.htm
http://www.geocities.com/Pentagon/2669/1abd.html
http://www.1stavn.com
http://www.cilledaire.org/SuperPrimum/dead (*now shut down*)
http://www.vvm.com/~firstcav/home.html
http://www.bullwhipsquadron.org/
http://www.9thcav.com/
http://bravotroop.my100megs.com/
http://cavalier44.my100megs.com/
http://www.bluemax-ara-assoc.com/
http://www.vhfcn.org/227hist.html
http://www.229thavbn.com/
http://www.smilingtigers.org
http://www.h-10th-cav.org/
http://www.members.tripod.com/JohnGriffith/AirCav.html
http://home.sprintmail.com/~karig/realcav.html
http://www.vietnamproject.ttu.edu/Banshee/
http://www.3rdsq17thacr.org/
http://www.ruthlessriders.net/
http://members.aol.com/BluGhstGrn/odgreen.html
http://www.blueghosts.com/
http://25thaviation.org/

http://www.raydon.com/48ahc/
http://web2.airmail.net/glad13/
http://www.114thaviationcompany.com/
http://www.129th.net/
http://www.vietnamexp.com/Robinhoods/RHMenu.htm
http://175thoutlaws.com/
http://www.187thahc.net/
http://238awc.org/
http://home.elp.rr.com/pinkpanthers/
http://www.77fa.org/
http://www.army.mil/cmh-pg/documents/vietnam/vni/249.htm
http://www.splorg.org/vietnam/orll.html
http://www.vietvet.org/aarpt1.htm
http://www.geocities.com/Pentagon/2669/0060mc.html
http://blackhawksusa.com
http://www.brianwizard.com/145/history/NL09HIST.html
http://www.afa.org/magazine/valor/0293valor.html
http://www.thebattleofkontum.com/bttlbgn.html
http://www.a101avn.org/AVIATIONUNITS1970.htm
http://www.geocities.com/Pentagon/Quarters/4668/ctrp.htm
http://incolor.inetnebr.com/iceman/CHECKLIST/checklist/index.htm
http://www.cantho-rvn.org/main.html
http://rattlers.org/heli-vets/
http://home.jps.net/~dhcntrl/
http://firemission.s5.com/
http://www.geocities.com/Pentagon/2669/0235mc.html
http://www.quad-a.org/Hall_of_Fame/seneff.htm
http://www.moorej.org/delta-discuss-avn/_disc/000000e0.htm
http://www.lighthorseaircav.com/
http://www.screamingeagle.org/hatley.htm
http://www.homeofheroes.com/moh/citations_1960_vn/langhorn_garfield.html
http://www.war-stories.com/mean-mr-mustard.htm
http://www.skytroopers.org/pace_of_ground_activity_slackens.htm
http://www.229thavbn.com/C229th/
http://www.vietnamproject.ttu.edu/banshee/trora.html
http://www.quartercav.net/

Other Media:
Vietnam Helicopter Pilots Association Database, which includes the US Army Gold Book data on all helicopters that served in Vietnam, and the VHPA histories for Operation *Lam Son 719* and the 1972 North Vietnamese Easter Offensive.

Documents:
All primary documents, including unit memoranda, operational lessons learned, Bell Technical reports and other miscellaneous documentation can be found at the Texas Tech University Vietnam Archives website: www.vietnam.ttu.edu

Unit Histories
C Battery, 4/77 Aerial Rocket Artillery, 101st Airborne Division – 1969-70
B Company, 4th Aviation Battalion, 4th Infantry Division – 1970
361st AeroWeapons Company – 1970
A Troop 7/17 Cavalry Squadron – 1970
129th Assault Helicopter Company – 1972
D Troop, 1/4th Cavalry Squadron – 1969
60th Assault Helicopter Company – 1971
1st Cavalry Division – 1965-69
101st Airborne Division – 1969
1st Infantry Division – 1965-69
F/79 AFA – 1971-72

PILOTS AND CREW CHIEFS INTERVIEWED

George Alexander	C/2/20 ARA
Roscoe Armstrong	35th AWC
Bob Baker	114th AHC
David Berry	114th AHC
John Baumhackl	11th ACR
Lou Bouault	B/1 AVN BN
George Brown	D/229 AHB
Mike Brown	F/79 AFA
Greg Bucy	B/25 AVN
Damon Cecil	C/7/1 CAV
Len Constantine	A/2/17 CAV, B/7/1 CAV
John Craig	C/1/9 CAV
Carl Crisp	114th AHC
Dick Dato	A/2/17 CAV
Joel Dummer	11th ACR
Dave Fuller	A/4/77 ARA
Gary Gardina	C/16 CAV
Paul Garrity	C/2/20 ARA
Gene Gawthrop	D/158 AHB
Bill Haponski	1/4th CAV
Pete Harlem	D/227 AHB
Bill Heilman	C/7/1 CAV
Jack Hepler	A/2/17 CAV
Gary Higgins	361st AWC
Jim Holt	11th ACR
Bill Jeanes	129th AHC
Ken Jeche l	B/1 AVN
Walker Jones	C/1/9 CAV
Gene Kennedy	238th AWC
Randy Kunkelman	B/2/17 CAV
Ron Leonard	B/25 AVN
John Malowney	A/3/17, B/7/1
Barry Martens	A/4/77 ARA
'Mac' McCloy	C/1/9 CAV
Matt McKnight	11th ACR
Hugh Mills	D/1/4 CAV, D/3/5 CAV, C/16 CAV
Jim Moran	C/2/20 ARA
Steve Nash	A/2/17 CAV
John Powell	1/9 CAV
Jim Preston	7/1 CAV, 5 AVN DET (COBRA NETT)
Terry Queall	A/2/20 ARA
Bill Reeder	361st AWC
Jessie Robertson	334th AHC, B/2/17 CAV
Ken Rubin	334th AHC
Mike Scheuerman	361st AWC
Gary Schoonover	B/25 AVN
Rick Sciapiti	114th AHC
Dan Shaver	C/16 CAV
Steve Shepard	C/7/17 CAV
Jim Shugart	D/227 AHB, E/1/9 CAV
Forrest Snyder	361st AWC
Jim Stanley	175th AHC
Nick Stein	COBRA NETT
Russell Stewart	B/7/1 CAV
Dave Tela	A/3/17 CAV
Frank Thompson	2/17 MAINTENANCE
Kerry Wedwick	114th AHC
Robert Wiggins	F/8 CAV
Rodney Woods	187th AHC
Randy Zahn	C/1/9 CAV

INDEX

References to illustrations are shown in **bold**. Colour Plates are prefixed 'cp.' and Colour Section plates 'cs.', with page and caption locators in (brackets).